D1547357

PICKER'S
POCKET·GUIDE

MAR   2015

BOTTLES

How to **Pick Antiques** like a Pro

MICHAEL POLAK

Published by

Krause Publications, a division of F+W, A Content + eCommerce Company
700 East State Street • Iola, WI 54990-0001
715-445-2214 • 888-457-2873
www.krausebooks.com

To order books or other products call toll-free 1-800-258-0929
or visit us online at www.krausebooks.com

Pictured on the cover: Top row, from left: an ink bottle (see P. 124), a George Washington bust flask (see P. 92), and a trio of whiskey bottles (see P. 176); bottom row, from left: label under glass flask, "Performing Bathing Beauty," clear glass, 6", half-pint, screw-on lid, American 1900-1920, $200-225; a bitters bottle (see P. 70), a Hutchinson bottle (see P. 119), and a poison bottle (see P. 148).

ISBN-13: 978-1-4402-4324-0
ISBN-10: 1-4402-4324-7

Designed by: Jana Iappa
Edited by: Kristine Manty

Printed in China

CONTENTS

Acknowledgments

Thanks to the following:

Jim Hagenbuch, Jessie Sailer, and Josh Reinhart of Glass Works Auctions (www.glswrk-auction.com) for the great assortment of photographs, pricing and background information, and overall support.

Hawaiian Bottle Club (Mike Leong, Brennan Leong, and Brandon Lee) and the entire club for the great assortment of photographs, description of Hawaiian bottles, and the valuable background information.

David Graci for his contribution of photographs and background information on soda and beer bottle closures.

Gary and Vickie Lewis for their contribution of photographs of applied color label soda bottles.

My wife, Jacque Pace Polak, for her continued patience and moral support.

Steve Ritter (Steve Ritter Auctioneering) for help in obtaining the applied color label soda bottle photographs and pricing inputs.

My daughter, Jennifer Stewart, for helping me during the long photo sessions and for your support of the project.

Rick Sweeney for his help and understanding with the pricing inputs for applied color label soda bottles.

John Tutton for the great milk bottle illustrations and overall support.

National Bottle Museum for support and contributions to the hobby of bottle collecting, and valuable input on the history of mineral and soda water bottle glass houses.

Violin Bottle Collectors Association and members for the contribution of photographs and an overall understanding of violin bottles. A special thank you to Bob Linden, Frank Bartlett, Samia Koudsi, and Bob Moore for their time and effort in providing photographs, pricing data, and resource information, Western bottle photographs and overall support of the project.

Jeff Wichman – American Bottle Auction (www.american-bottle.com) for providing a great assortment of bottle photographs and background and pricing information.

Norm Heckler Auctions (www.hecklerauction.com) –Thank you for the photo contributions and the background information, as well as your overall support.

Introduction

Welcome to the fun hobby of antique bottle collecting with the exciting new edition of the *Picker's Pocket Guide: Bottles*.

I thank all my readers for their support in making the *Antique Trader Bottles Identification & Price Guide* and *Warman's Bottles Field Guide* such huge successes. With the publication of each edition of those books, the positive response continues to be overwhelming. Living up to the nickname "The Bottle Bible" given to *Antique Trader Bottles Identification & Price Guide*, I've incorporated this positive feedback into the new *Picker's Pocket Guide: Bottles* as well.

The idea behind this new book, while continuing to be a detailed and informative reference guide, is to feature an expanded "Bottle Sources" section, starting on P. 42, to help pickers, and collectors, focus on where to "pick" all types of bottles. This section provides in-depth information not only on where to find and pick bottles, but also how to navigate through flea markets, thrift stores, bottle shows, antiques stores, and other hotspots for those hidden bottle treasures. In addition, this pocket guide also includes a "Digging for Bottles" section on P. 182 that specifically targets where and how to find bottles by digging, since that is a great way to pick bottles. And to better understand the details of how to price and evaluate a bottle, check out the section on P. 39 titled "Determining Bottle Values."

Overall, there are 17 chapters of bottles—including Bitters, Black Glass, Flasks, Fire Grenades, Soda, and Whiskey—that provide beginning and veteran pickers and collectors with a broad range of information and reference data. The book also includes extensive sections on the history and origin of glass and bottles; how a beginner gets started; bottle basics, bottle handling techniques, and other reference material. In addition to a number of valuable illustrations, this edition also features stunning color photographs throughout the book.

Interest in bottle collecting continues to grow, with new bottle clubs forming throughout the United States and Europe, and pickers will get tips on what bottles interest these collectors. More pickers, as well as collectors, are spending their free time digging through old dumps and foraging through

These extremely rare history flasks rocked the world of antique bottle collectors when they sold at auction for world-record prices. The sapphire blue "General Washington" firecracker flask, at right, sold for **$101,620**. The yellow green "General Jackson and Bust" portrait flask, below, sold for **$176,670.** Another Washington flask also sold for a record price; see P. 92 for more information.

Norm Heckler Auctions

ghost towns, digging out old outhouses (that's right), exploring abandoned mine shafts, and searching their favorite bottle or antiques shows, swap meets, flea markets, and garage sales. In addition, the Internet has greatly expanded, offering numerous opportunities and resources to buy and sell bottles with many new auction websites, without leaving the house. Many bottle clubs now have websites providing even more information for the collector. These new technologies and resources have helped the hobby of bottle collecting continue to grow and gain interest.

Most collectors, however, still look beyond the type and value of a bottle into its origin and history. I find that researching the history of a bottle is *almost* as interesting a project as finding the bottle itself. I enjoy both pursuits for their close ties to the rich history of the settling of the United States and the early methods of merchandising.

My goal has always been to enhance the hobby of bottle collecting for both beginning and expert collectors and to help them experience the excitement of collecting, especially the thrill of making a special find. I hope this book brings you an increased understanding and enjoyment of the hobby of bottle collecting. Now, grab your copy of *Picker's Pocket Guide: Bottles*, toss it into your backpack, purse, or pocket, and check out some bottles.

To provide input regarding this first edition, to order books, or just talk about bottles, contact me at bottleking@earthlink.net or visit my website, www.bottlebible.com. Good bottle hunting and have fun with the hobby of bottle collecting.

— *Michael Polak*

How to Use This Book

Picker's Pocket Guide: Bottles is formatted to assist all collectors and pickers, from the novice to the seasoned veteran, in finding elusive and hidden bottles. The table of contents indicates these sections such as "Beginning Tips," that veterans may want to skip. However, other sections, including "History and Origin," "Bottle Basics," "Bottle Sources," "Bottle Handling," and "Digging for Bottles," will provide additional valuable information and resources for the benefit of all.

The main section of the book including 17 chapters on various kinds of bottles covers old bottles manufactured almost exclusively before 1900, broken down into categories based on physical type and the bottle's original contents. Where applicable, trade names are listed alphabetically within these sections. In some categories, such as flasks, trade names were not embossed on the bottles, so pieces are listed by embossing or other identification that appears on the bottle. Descriptive terms used to identify these pieces are explained in the introductory sections and are also listed in the glossary at the end of the book.

The reference and research sections, "Trademark Identification," and "Museum and Research Resource," provide additional assistance and help to all collectors and pickers.

History and Origin

Glass bottles are not as new as some people believe. In fact, the glass bottle has been around for about 3,000 years. During the 2nd century B.C., Roman glass was free-blown with metal blowpipes and shaped with tongs that were used to change the shape of the bottle or vessel. The finished item was then decorated with enameling and engraving. The Romans even get credit for originating what we think of today as the basic "store bottle" and early merchandising techniques.

In the late 1st century B.C., the Romans, with the assistance of glassworker craftsmen from Syria and Egypt, began making glass vials that local doctors and pharmacists used to dispense pills, healing powders and miscellaneous potions. The vials were three to four inches long and narrow. The majority of early bottles made after the Romans were sealed with a cork or a glass stopper, whereas Romans used a small stone rolled in tar as their stopper. The finished vials contained many impurities such as sand particles and bubbles because of the crude manufacturing process. The thickness of the glass and the crude finish, however, made Roman glass very resilient compared to the glass of later times, which accounts for the survival and good preservation of some Roman bottles as old as 2,500 years. The Roman glass techniques and manufacturing methods would eventually influence all of the European Art and Industrial complexes.

The first attempt to manufacture glass in America is thought to have taken place at the Jamestown settlement in Virginia around 1608 by the London Company. It is interesting to note that the majority of glass produced in Jamestown was earmarked for shipment back to England (due to its lack of resources) and not for the new settlements. As it turned out, the Jamestown glass house enterprise ended up a failure almost before it got started. The poor quality of glass produced and the small quantity simply couldn't support England's needs.

While a second unsuccessful attempt (in lieu of "pattern") was made in 1621, the first successful American glasshouse was opened in 1739 in New Jersey by Caspar Wistar, a brass button manufacturer who immigrated from Germany to

Roman bottles, jars, and glass objects, 1st-3rd century A.D., found in the baths and necropolises of Cimiez Nice, France.

Philadelphia in 1717. During a trip in Salem County, New Jersey, Wistar noticed the abundance of white sand along with the proximity of clay, wood and water transportation. He soon bought 2,000 acres of the heavily wooded land and made arrangements for experienced glass workers to come from Europe; the factory was completed in the fall of 1739.

Since English law did not permit the colonists to manufacture anything in competition with England, Wistar kept a low profile. In fact, most of what was written during the factory's operation implied that it was less than successful. Caspar Wistar died in 1752 a very wealthy man and left the factory to his son, Richard. The Wistar glass operation, however, closed in 1779 as a result of lost markets, a result of the Revolutionary War.

Henry Stiegel started the next major glasshouse operation in Manheim, Pa., between 1763 and 1774, and eventually went on to establish several more. The Pitkin Glass Works was opened in East Hartford, Conn., around 1783 and was the first American glasshouse to provide figured flasks and also the most successful of its time until it closed around 1830 due to the high cost of wood for fuel. By 1850, there were approximately 40 glass manufacturing factories in New York alone, producing millions of bottles and jars.

To understand the early successes and far more numerous failures of early glasshouses, it is essential that the reader get an overview of the challenges that glass workers faced in acquiring raw materials and constructing the glasshouse. The glass factory of the 19th century was usually built near abundant sources of sand, wood or coal and close to numerous roads, rivers and other waterways for transportation of raw materials and finished products to the major Eastern markets of Boston, New York, and Philadelphia. Finding a suitable location was usually not a problem, but once production was underway, resources quickly diminished.

The majority of furnaces burned wood until the middle of the 19th century. The first American glasshouse to use soft coal was built by Isaac Craig and James O'Hara at Pittsburgh in 1776-1797. Bituminous coal became available after 1810, and during the 1850s anthracite was used. By 1860, only one furnace in New England continued to burn wood, and by 1880, the fuel used in glass making in the United States was mainly coal. The next major problem was constructing the glasshouse building, a large wooden structure housing a primitive furnace that was about nine feet in diameter and shaped like a beehive.

A major financial drain on the glass companies—and one of the causes of so many of the businesses failing—was the large melting pots inside the furnace that held the molten glass. The melting pot, which cost about $100 and took eight months to build, was formed by hand from a long coil of clay and was the only substance known that would not melt when the glass was heated to 2,700 degrees F. The pots lasted about eight weeks, as exposure to high temperature over a long period of time caused the clay itself to turn to glass. The cost of regularly replacing melting pots proved to be the downfall of many an early glass factory.

Throughout the 19th century, glasshouses opened and closed because of changes in demand and technological improvements. Between 1840 and 1890, an enormous demand for glass containers developed to satisfy the demands of the whiskey, beer, medical, and food packing industries. Largely

MOST SOUGHT-AFTER BOTTLES

In 1862, Carlton Newman and Patrick Brennan founded Pacific Glass Works in San Francisco. In 1876, San Francisco Glass Works bought Pacific Glass Works and renamed the company San Francisco and Pacific Glass Works (SFPGW). Today these early bottles manufactured in San Francisco are the most desired by Western collectors.

due to this steady demand, glass manufacturing in the United States evolved into a stable industry. Western expansion and the great gold and silver rush between 1850 and 1860 contributed a great deal to this increase in demand.

While the Eastern glasshouses had been in production since 1739, the West didn't begin its entry into glass manufacturing until 1858 when Baker & Cutting started the first glasshouse in San Francisco. Until then, the West depended on glass bottles from the East. The glass manufactured by Baker & Cutting, however, was considered to be poor quality, and production was eventually discontinued.

In 1862, Carlton Newman and Patrick Brennan founded Pacific Glass Works in San Francisco. In 1876, San Francisco Glass Works bought Pacific Glass Works and renamed the company San Francisco and Pacific Glass Works (SFPGW). Today these early bottles manufactured in San Francisco are the most desired by Western collectors.

Unlike other businesses of the time that saw major changes in manufacturing processes, producing the glass bottles remained unchanged. The process gave each bottle character, producing unique shapes, imperfections, irregularities, and various colors.

That all changed at the turn of the century when Michael J. Owens invented the first fully automated bottle making machine. Although many fine bottles were manufactured between 1900-1930, Owens' invention ended an era of unique bottle design that no machine process could ever duplicate.

To better understand the history and origin of antique bottles, it is important to take a look at the development of the manufacturing process.

FREE BLOWN BOTTLES: B.C.-1860 (FIGURE 1, P. 14)

Around the 1st century B.C., the blowpipe, a long hollow metal rod, was invented. The tip was dipped into molten glass and the glass blower blew into the rod to form the molten glass into the desired form, bowls, and other glass containers.

PONTIL MARKS: 1618-1866

Once the bottle was blown, it was removed from the rod through the use of a three-foot metal pontil rod that was dipped into the tank of molten glass and applied to the bottom of the bottle. The neck of the bottle was then touched with a wet rod to break it from the blowpipe. There are four general types of pontil marks:

- **Glass Tipped or Open Pontil** – This type of pontil mark was left by the use of a solid iron bar as the pontil rod, leaving a jagged broken glass circular scar on the bottom of the bottle.
- **Blowpipe or Ring Pontil** – This mark was created similar to the glass-tipped pontil. It was thought that it was less expensive to just use another blowpipe as the pontil.
- **Sand Pontil** – This mark is created when the glass blower dips the glass tipped pontil in sand before attaching to the bottom of the bottle. This was done to keep the pontil rod from sticking to the bottle and making removal easier.
- **Bare Iron Pontil** – One of the most sought after bottles has the "iron" pontil mark. The residual red, reddish black, gray or black deposits are iron, usually oxidized iron, or commonly know as "rust."

1 The blowpipe was inserted into the pot of hot "metal" (liquid glass) and twisted to gather the requisite amount onto the end of the pipe.

2 The blowpipe was then rolled slowly on a metal table to allow the red-hot glass to cool slightly on the outside and to sag.

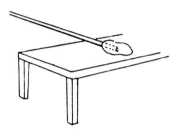

3 The blower then blew into the pipe to form an internal central bubble.

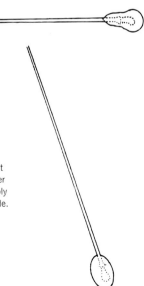

4 The glass was further expanded and sometimes turned in a wooden block that had been dipped in cold water to prevent charring, or possibly rolled again on the metal table.

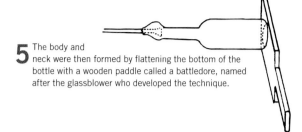

5 The body and
neck were then formed by flattening the bottom of the
bottle with a wooden paddle called a battledore, named
after the glassblower who developed the technique.

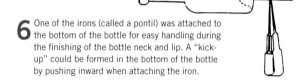

6 One of the irons (called a pontil) was attached to
the bottom of the bottle for easy handling during
the finishing of the bottle neck and lip. A "kick-
up" could be formed in the bottom of the bottle
by pushing inward when attaching the iron.

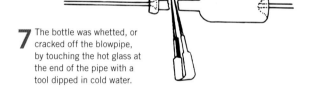

7 The bottle was whetted, or
cracked off the blowpipe,
by touching the hot glass at
the end of the pipe with a
tool dipped in cold water.

8 With the bottle held on a pontil, the
blower reheated the neck to polish the
lip and further smoothed it by tooling.
Bottles were created with a variety of
applied and tooled ring and collar tops.

SNAP CASES: 1860-1903 (FIGURE 2)

Between 1850 and 1860, the snap case was developed to replace the pontil rod. This represented the first major invention for bottle making since the blowpipe. The snap case was a five-foot metal rod that had claws to grasp the bottle. A snap locked the claw into place in order to hold the bottle more securely while the neck was being finished. Each snap case was tailor-made to fit bottles of a certain size and shape. These bottles have no pontil scars or marks, which left the bases of the bottle free for lettering or design. There may, however, be some minor grip marks on the side as a result of the claw device.

The snap case instrument was used for small mouth bottle production until the automatic bottle machine came into existence in 1903.

FIG. 2: SNAP CASES: 1860-1903

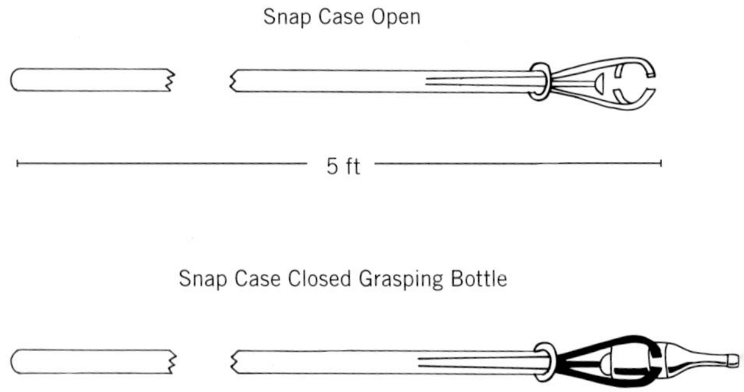

Snap Case Open

|——————————— 5 ft ———————————|

Snap Case Closed Grasping Bottle

MOLDED BOTTLES: B.C.-1900 (FIGURE 3, P. 18)

The use of molds in bottle making, which really took hold in the early 1800s, actually dates back to the 1st century with the Romans. As detailed earlier in the free-blown process, the glass blower shaped the bottle, or vessel, by blowing and turning it in the air. When using a mold, the glass blower would then take a few puffs while lowering the red-hot shaped mass into the hollow mold. The blower continued blowing air into the tube until the glass compressed itself against the sides of the mold to acquire the finished shape. Most of these bottle molds were made of clay or wood, and formed only the base and body of the container. The neck had to be drawn out utilizing the skill of the glassblower.

Molds were usually made in two or more sections to enable the mold to come apart. The hardened bottle was then easily removed. Since it was impossible to create perfectly fitted molds, the seams showed on the surface of the finished article, providing a clue as to the manufacturing methods used in the production of the bottle. Molds were categorized as "open," in which only the body of the bottle was forced, with the neck and lip being added later, or "closed," in which the neck and lip were part of the original mold (Figure 3). The average life for a wooden mold was between 100 to 1,000 castings, depending of the thickness of the glass blown into them. The most common mold in use after 1860 was the cast iron mold, which proved to be the best and more economical way to manufacture cheap bottles.

By 1900, a number of improvements, such as tightly locking molds components, allowed for vent holes to be drilled into the mold to allow air within to escape while being replaced with hot glass. These vent holes were bored in the shoulders and bases of the mold. Then the hot glass penetrated part way into the holes, leaving a mark on the glass about the size of a pin head. These marks are very noticeable on the shoulder of quart whisky bottles of the 1900s. Often the vent mark was incorporated into the design on the bottles. Later two types of molds came into use:

(1) The three-piece mold, used between 1809 and 1880, which consisted of two main kinds: the three-piece dip mold and the full-height mold.

(2) The turn mold or paste mold, used between 1880 and 1900.

The introduction of the three-piece mold helped the bottle industry become stronger in the 19th century by increasing production to keep up with demand.

FIG.3: MOLDS: FIRST CENTURY B.C., 1900

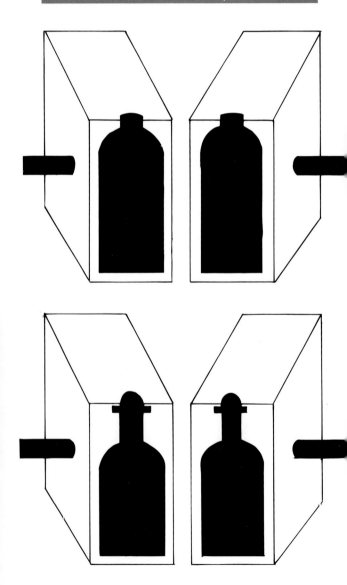

THREE-PIECE MOLDS (FIGURE 4)
THREE-PIECE DIP MOLD:

The bottom section of the bottle mold was one piece, while the top, from the shoulder up, was two separate pieces. The mold seams circled the bottle at the shoulder and on each side of the neck.

FIG.4: THREE-PIECE MOLD

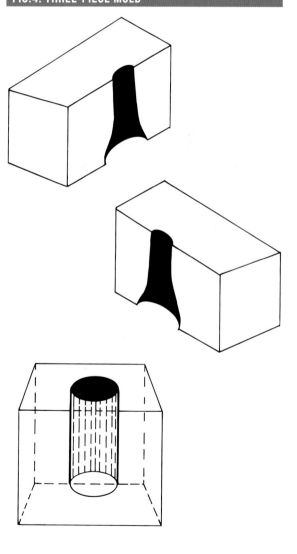

FULL HEIGHT MOLD:

The entire bottle was formed in the mold, forming vertical seams on both sides that ran from the bottom of the bottle to below the lip.

Full height metal mold: front view.

Full height metal mold: side view.

Full height metal bottle mold: "Quick Death – Insecticide – And Disinfectant – REG. U.S. Pat. Office – Victory – Chemical Co. – 312 No. 15th St. – Philada. Pa.," 1880-1900. Heavy hinged cylindrical metal mold with handles made to create bottles, top diameter 6" x 8-1/2", not including handles. Shown are an 1890 "Quick Death" bottle made from the mold, a bottle in the large size of the same product (this mold is in the collection of Richard Watson), a cobalt blue bottle blown recently by Frank Stebbens, and a "Dead Stuck for Bugs" bottle.

TURN MOLD OR PASTE MOLD

Wooden molds were kept wet to prevent the hot glass from igniting or charring the wood. Turning the bottle in the wet mold erased all seams and mold marks, and gave the glass a high luster. After metal molds replaced wooden molds, manufacturers used a paste inside the mold, allowing the bottle to slide easily during the turning process, which explains the origin of the terms "turn mold" and "paste mold."

MASON JARS: 1858

In 1858, John L. Mason invented the wide-mouth jar that became famous as a food preservative container. The new screw-top jar was formed in the same mold as the body. The jar was then broken from the blowpipe and sent to the annealing oven to temper the glass, making it more resistant to breakage. Then the jagged edges of the rims were ground down. Earlier jars can be distinguished from later ones by the rough and sharp edges produced by the grinding process.

PRESS AND BLOW PROCESS: 1892

In 1892, a semi-automatic process called "press and blow" was invented to produce wide-mouth containers such as fruit jars and milk bottles. First molten glass was pressed into the mold to form the mouth and lip. Then a metal plunger was inserted through the mouth and air pressure was applied to form the body of the bottle.

Press and blow milk mold used by Thatcher milk bottles, Lockport Glass Company, Lockport, N.Y., circa 1927.

THE AUTOMATIC BOTTLE-MAKING MACHINE: 1903

Michael J. Owens, recognized as the inventor of the first automatic bottle-making machine, started as a glass blower in 1874 at the young age of 15. Owens proved to be a capable inventor and in 1888, while working in Toledo, Ohio, for the American Lamp Chimney Company, he invented a semi-automatic machine for tumblers and lantern chimneys. Utilizing his engineering talent and his glassmaking experience, he developed his first bottle-making machine in 1899 (Figure 1). After experimenting with three machines, he perfected the process with his fourth in 1903 (Figures 2, 3, and 4). Owens continued to make additional improvements and introduced Machine No. 5 (Figure 5) in 1904. This final improvement allowed the continuous movement of the machine that eliminated the intermittent stopping of the rotation of both machine and glass tank and increased the quantity and quality of bottles. A major advantage with these new machines was that the neck and top of the bottle no longer required hand finishing.

At first Owens' machine made only heavy bottles because they were in the greatest demand but, in 1909, improvements to the machine made it possible to produce small prescription bottles. Between 1909 and 1917, numerous other automatic bottle-making machines were invented, and soon all bottles were formed automatically throughout the world.

In 1904, Owens' first machine produced 13,000 bottles a day. By 1917, machine No. 5 was producing approximately 60,000 bottles a day. In 1917, the "gob feeder" was developed, which produced a measured amount of molten glass from which a bottle could be blown. In this process, a gob of glass is drawn from the tank and cut off by shears.

Early in 1910, the Owens Bottle Company installed an automatic conveyor system in its factories, eliminating the need for "carry in" boys who gathered bottles from the machine and carried them to the annealer oven.

The Original Owens Process
The basic invention of the Owens Bottle Machine is fixed on this crude vacuum device. The story fully describes the method of operation.

1 **The Original Owens Process:** The basic invention of the Owens Bottle Machine is fixed on this crude vacuum device.

Machine No. 2
This machine is similar in construction to the original device, except that it is mounted on an upright column, with a wheelbase to move the machine forward to and back from the glass pot.

Machine No. 3
This was the first rotating machine, and was very novel in construction. It was for the requirements of this machine that the revolving glass tank was developed.

2 **Machine No. 2:** This machine is similar in construction to the original device, except that it is mounted on an upright column, with a wheelbase to move the machine forward to and back from the glass pot.

3 **Machine No. 3:** This was the first rotating machine, and was novel in construction. It was for the requirements of this machine that the revolving glass tank was developed.

Machine No. 4
This machine was the outgrowth of the great encouragement Mr. Owens received from the operation of No. 3, and at the time it was built was considered a marvelous specimen of engineering skill.

Machine No. 5
This machine shows a great improvement over No. 4. It formed the foundation for the general type in use at the present day.

4 **Machine No. 4:** This machine was the outgrowth of the great encouragement Mr. Owens received from the operation of No. 3, and at the time it was built was considered a marvelous specimen of engineering skill.

5 **Machine No. 5:** This machine shows a great improvement over No. 4. It formed the foundation for the general type in use at the present day.

SCREW-TOPPED BOTTLES

One last note about bottle making concerns the process of producing screw-topped bottles. Early glass blowers produced bottles with inside and outside screw caps long before the bottle making machines mechanized the process. Because early methods of production were so complex, screw-topped bottles produced before the 1800s were considered specialty bottles and expensive to replace. Today they are considered to be rare and collectible. In fact, the conventional screw-top bottle did not become common until after 1924 when the glass industry standardized the threads.

Beginning Tips

The first thing to understand about antique bottle collecting is that there aren't set rules. Your finances, spare time, storage space, and preferences will influence your approach. As a collector or picker, you need to think about whether to specialize and focus on a specific type of bottle or group of bottles or become a maverick who acquires everything. The majority of bottle collectors that I have known, including me, took the maverick approach as new collectors. We grabbed everything in sight, ending up with bottles of every type, shape, and color.

After 40 years of collecting, I recommend that beginners only do a small amount of maverick collecting and focus on a specific group of bottles. Taking the general approach gave me a broader background of knowledge about bottles and glass, but specializing provides the following distinct advantages:

- More time for organization, study, and research
- The ability to become an authority in a particular area
- The opportunity to trade with other specialists who may have duplicate or unwanted bottles
- The ability to negotiate a better deal by spotting underpriced bottles

Specialized collectors will still be tempted by bottles that don't quite fit into their collection, so they will cheat a little and give in to the maverick urge. This occasional cheating sometimes results in a smaller side collection, or turns the collector back to being a maverick. Remember, there are no set rules except to have fun.

STARTING A COLLECTION

What does it cost to start a collection and how do you know the value of a bottle? The beginner can do well with just a few pointers. Let's start with buying bottles, instead of digging for bottles. This is a quicker approach for the new bottle collector.

WHAT SHOULD I PAY?

Over the years, I've developed a quick method of buying bottles by grouping them into three categories:

• LOW END OR COMMON BOTTLES

These bottles have noticeable wear and are never

embossed. The labels are typically missing or not visible. In most cases, the labels are completely gone. The bottles are dirty and not easily cleaned. They have some scrapes but are free of chips. These bottles are usually clear.

• AVERAGE GRADE/COMMON BOTTLES

These bottles show some wear and labels may be visible but are usually faded. They are generally clear or aqua and free of scrapes or chips. Some of these bottles may have minimal embossing, but not likely.

• HIGH END AND UNIQUE BOTTLES

These bottles can be empty or partially or completely full and have the original stoppers and labels or embossing. Bottles can be clear but are usually green, teal blue, yellow, or yellow green with no chips or scrapes and very little wear. If a bottle has been stored in a box, it is most likely in good or excellent condition. Also, the box must be in very good condition.

Price ranges will be discussed briefly here since there is a separate "Determining Bottle Values" section. Usually, low-end bottles can be found for $1 to $5, average from $5 to $20, and high-end from $20 to $100, although some high-end bottles sell for $1, 000 or more. Any bottles above $100 should be closely examined by an experienced and knowledgeable collector.

As a general rule, I try not to spend more than $2 per bottle for low-end bottles and $5-$7 for average. It's easier to stick to this guideline when you've done your homework, but sometimes you just get lucky. As an example, during a number of bottle and antiques shows, I have found sellers who had grab bags full of bottles for $2 a bag. I never pass up a bargain like this because of the lure of potential treasures. After one show, I discovered a total of nine bottles, some purple, all earlier than 1900 and in great shape with embossing, for a total cost of 22 cents per bottle. What could be better than that? Well, I found a Tonopah, Nevada, medicine valued at $100.

In the high-end category, deals are usually made after some good old horse trading and bartering. But, hey, that's part of the fun. Always let the seller know that you are a new collector with a limited budget. It really helps. Bottle sellers will almost always help new collectors get the best deal on a limited budget.

IS IT OLD OR NEW?

Collectors and pickers should also know the difference between old and new bottles. Quite often, people new to the hobby assume that any old bottle is an antique, and if a bottle isn't old, it isn't collectible. With bottle collecting, that isn't necessarily the case. In the antiques world, an antique is defined as an article more than 100 years old, but a number of bottles listed in this book that are less than 100 years old are just as valuable—and perhaps more so—than those that by definition are antiques.

The number and variety of old and antique bottles is greater than the new collectible items in today's market. On the other hand, the Jim Beam, Ezra Brooks, Avon, recent Coca-Cola, figural, and miniature soda and liquor bottles manufactured more recently are very desirable and collectible and are manufactured for that purpose. If you decide you want to collect new bottles, the best time to buy is when the first issue comes out on the market. When the first issues are gone, the collector market is the only available source, which limits availability and drives up prices considerably.

For all collectors and pickers, books, references guides, magazines, and other similar literature are readily available at libraries, in bookstores, and on the Internet.

BEWARE OF REPRODUCTIONS AND REPAIRS

I want to emphasize the importance of being aware of reproductions and repaired bottles. Always check bottles, jars, and pottery carefully to make sure that there have been no repairs or special treatments. It's best to hold the item up to the light or take it outside with the dealer to look for cracks, nicks, or dings. Also, look for scratches that may have occurred during cleaning. Also check the closures. Having the proper closure can make a big difference in the value of a bottle, so it's important to make sure the closure fits securely, and the metal lid is stamped with the correct patent dates or lettering. If you need help, ask an experienced collector, and if you have any doubt about a bottle's authenticity, request that the dealer provide a money-back guarantee.

Check out antique and bottle shows, flea markets, swap meets, garage sales, and antique shops. Pick up those bottles, ask plenty of questions, and you will be surprised by how much you'll learn and how much fun you'll have.

Bottle Basics

New bottle pickers need to learn certain facts such as age identification, grading, labeling, glass imperfections, and peculiarities.

AGE

The common methods of determining age are mold seams, lips/tops, stoppers/closures, and color variations.

• MOLD SEAMS

Prior to 1900, bottle manufacturing was done by either a blowpipe (free blown) to 1860 or with a mold to 1900. The mouth or lip was formed last and applied to the bottle after completion (applied lip). The applied lip can be identified by the mold seam that runs from the base up to the neck, and near the end of the lip. For machine-made bottles, the lip is formed first and the mold seam runs over the lip. The closer the seam extends to the top of the bottle, the more recent the bottle.

On bottles manufactured before 1860, the mold seams end low on the neck or at the shoulder. Between 1860 and 1880, the mold seam stops right below the mouth and makes it easy to detect where the lip was separately formed. Around 1880, the closed mold was utilized, in which the neck and lip were mechanically shaped, and the glass was severed from the blowpipe with the ridge being evened off by hand sanding or filing. This mold seam usually ends within one-quarter inch from the top of the bottle. After 1900, the seam extends all the way to the top.

• LIPS AND TOPS

One of the best ways to identify bottles manufactured prior to 1840 is by the presence of a "sheared lip." This type of lip was formed by cutting or snipping the glass free of the blowpipe with a pair of shears that left the lip with a stovepipe look.

Around 1840, bottle manufacturers began to apply a glass ring around the sheared lip, forming a "laid-on-ring" lip. Between 1840 and 1880, numerous variations of lips or tops were produced using a variety of tools. After 1880, manufacturers started to pool their processing information, resulting in more evenly finished and uniform tops. As a general rule, the more uneven and crude the lip or top, the older the bottle.

Above are just four examples of the myriad types of lips and tops created on antique bottles.

FIG. 1: TOOLED BOTTLE LIPS/TOPS IDENTIFICATION

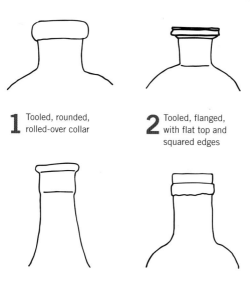

1 Tooled, rounded, rolled-over collar

2 Tooled, flanged, with flat top and squared edges

3 Tooled, rounded above 3/4" flat band

4 Tooled, flat ring below thickening plain lip

5 Tooled, narrow beveled fillet below thickened plain lip

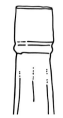

6 Tooled, broad sloping collar above beveled ring

7 Tooled, plain broad sloping collar

8 Tooled, broad sloping collar with beveled edges at top and bottom

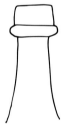

9 Tooled, broad flat collar sloping to heavy rounded ring

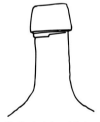

10 Tooled, broad flat vertical collar with uneven lower edge

11 Tooled, double rounded collar, upper deeper than lower; neck slightly pinched at base of collar

12 Tooled, broad round collar with lower level

FIG. 2: BOTTLE LIPS/OTHER TOPS IDENTIFICATION

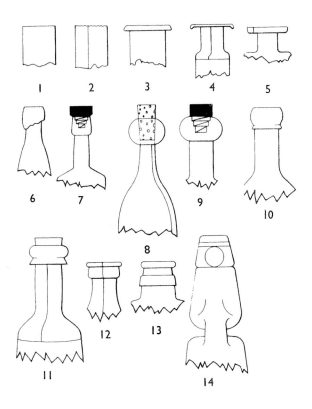

1. Free-blown
2. Sheared
3. Rolled
4. Flared
5. Laid-on ring
6. Applied top
7. Internal threads
8. Blob-top (cork use)
9. Blob-top (internal thread)
10. Improved applied lip on the two-piece mold bottle
11. Improved applied lip on a three-piece mold bottle
12. 20th century lip
13. Collar below lip
14. Hiram Codd lip

• CLOSURES/STOPPERS

The Romans used small stones rolled in tar as stoppers, and for many centuries there was little advancement. For most of the 15th and 16th centuries, the closure consisted of a sized cloth tied down with heavy thread or string. The stopper beneath the cover was made of wax or bombase (cotton wadding). Cotton wool was also dipped in wax and used as a stopper along with coverings of parchment, paper, or leather. Corks and glass stoppers were used in great numbers, with the cork sometimes being tied or wired down for effervescent liquids. When the "closed mold" came into existence, the shape of the lip was more accurately controlled, making it possible to invent capping devices.

On July 23, 1872, British inventor Hiram Codd invented a bottle made with a groove inside the neck and was granted Patent No. 129,652. A glass marble was inserted and then a ring of cork or rubber was fitted into the groove. When an effervescing liquid was used, the pressure of the gas forced the marble to the top of the neck, sealing the bottle. A second patent, Patent No. 138,230, issued April 29, 1873, contained an interior lug, a ball-holding element. Interestingly, many young boys broke these bottles to get the marble.

Glass stoppers from 1850 to 1900.

Hiram Codd interior ball stopper, Patent #129,652, July 23, 1872. Carbonation pushed the glass ball to the top of the neck, forming a tight seal.

Charles G. Hutchinson stopper, Patent #213,992, April 8, (year uncertain). A wire loop was pulled upward to seat a rubber gasket in the neck of the bottle. Carbonation helped keep it in place.

From 1879 to the early 1900s, the Hutchinson stopper was a common bottle closure after Patent No. 213,992 was issued on April 8, 1879. Hutchinson's concept used a heavy wire loop to control a rubber gasket that stayed inside the neck of the bottle. After filling the bottle, the gasket was pulled up against the shoulders and was kept in place by the carbonation. The Hutchinson stopper was easily adaptable to a number of other bottle types.

Until the invention of the crown cap in 1892, the lightning stopper was the best closure for beer bottles. The lightning stopper was a porcelain or rubber plug anchored to the outside of the bottle by a permanently attached wire. The wire formed a bar that controlled the opening and closing of the bottle.

In 1892, William Painter patented the crown cap, which consisted of a metal and cork gasket crimped over the mouth of the bottle. This cap revolutionized the soft drink and beer bottling industry. By 1915, all major bottlers had switched to the crown-type cap. Finally, in 1902, threads were manufactured on the outside of the lip to enable a threaded cap to be screwed onto the mouth of the bottle. This wasn't a new idea. Early glass blowers produced bottles with inside and outside screw caps long before the bottle-making machines. Early methods of production were so complex, however, that screw-topped bottles produced before the 1800s were considered specialty bottles.

They were expensive to replace and today are considered rare and quite collectible. The conventional screw-top bottle did not become common until after 1924, when the glass industry standardized the threads.

In 1875, some glass manufacturers introduced an inside screw-neck whiskey bottle using a rubber stopper. This invention wasn't popular because the alcohol interacted with the rubber, which discolored the whiskey and made it bitter.

The lightning stopper, designed to hold carbonated beverages, was eventually replaced by the crown cap.

William Painter crown cap, Patent #468,226, Feb. 2, 1892.

Dumfries Ale (English). The bottle's inside threads were sealed with a rubber stopper. This device was unpopular because the rubber interacted with the contents, distorting its color and taste.

The following list is a portion of the brands of embossed whiskeys that featured the inside threaded neck and the approximate dates of manufacture:

WHISKEY COMPANY	DATE OF CIRCULATION
Adolph Harris	1907-1912
Chevalier Castle	1907-1910
Crown (squatty)	1905-1912
Crown (pint)	1896-1899
Donnelly Rye	1910-1917
Old Gilt Edge	1907-1912
Roth (aqua)	1903-1911
Roth (amber sq.)	1898-1909
Roth (amber fluted shoulder)	1903-1911
Roth (amber qt.)	1903-1911
Rusconi-Fisher	1902-1915
Taussig (clear)	1915-1918

• GLASS COLOR

Another effective method of determining age is by glass color. Producing colored and clear glass were major challenges for all glass manufacturers. Prior to 1840, intentionally colored or colorless glass was reserved for fancy figured flasks and vessels. Bottle color was essentially considered unimportant until 1880, when food preservation packers began to demand clear glass for food products. Because most glass produced prior to this time was green, glass manufacturers began using manganese to bleach out the green tinge created by the iron content. Only then did clear bottles become common.

Iron slag was used up to 1860 and produced a dark olive green or olive amber glass that has become known as black glass and was used for wine and beverage bottles that needed protection from light. Colors natural to bottle glass are brown, amber, olive green, and aqua.

Blue, green, and purple were produced by metallic oxides added to the glass batch. Cobalt was added for blue glass; sulfur for yellow and green; manganese and nickel for purple; nickel for brown; copper or gold for red; and tin or zinc for milk-colored glass (for apothecary vials, druggist bottles, and pocket bottles).

The Hocking Glass Co. discovered a process for making a brilliant red glass described as copper-ruby. The color was

COLOR	PRODUCED BY ADDING OXIDE
Aqua	Iron oxide in sand
Black	Iron oxide, manganese, cobalt, iron
Clear	Selenium
Yellow	Nickel
Red	Gold, copper, or selenium
Blue	Cobalt oxide
Blue-Green	Iron in silicate-based glass
Amber	Manganese oxide, sulfur, carbon oxide
Dark Brown	Sulphide of copper and sulphide of sodium
Amethyst (Purple)	Sulphide of nickel
Rose Tinted	Adding selenium directly into the batch
Orange Red	Selenium mixed first with cadmium sulphide
Dark Reddish-Brown	Sodium sulphide
Reddish Yellow	Sulphide of sodium and molybdenite
Yellow Green	Uranium oxide
Green	Iron oxide
Milk Glass	Tin or zinc oxide
Olive Green	Iron oxide and black oxide of manganese
Purple	Manganese
Orange	Oxide of iron and manganese

achieved by adding copper oxide to a glass batch as it was cooling and then immediately reheating the batch before use. Since these bright colors were expensive to produce, they are very rare and sought after by most collectors. Many bottle collectors think purple is the most appealing color and therefore is prized above others. The iron contained in sand caused glass to take on color between green and blue. Glass manufacturers used manganese that counteracted the aqua to produce clear glass. But when exposed to ultraviolet light from the sun, the manganese in the glass oxidizes and turns the glass to purple. The longer the glass is exposed to the sunlight, the deeper the purple color. Glass with manganese content was most common in bottles produced between 1880 and 1914. Because Germany was the main producer of manganese, the supply ceased at the beginning of World War I. By 1916, the glass making industry began to use selenium as a neutralizing agent. Glass produced between 1914 and 1930 is most likely to change to an amber or straw color.

• IMPERFECTIONS

Imperfections and blemishes also provide clues to how old a bottle is and often add to the charm and value of an individual piece. Blemishes usually show up as bubbles or "seeds" in the glass. In the process of making glass, air bubbles form and rise to the surface where they pop. As the fining out (elimination process) became more advanced around 1920, these bubbles or seeds were eliminated.

Another peculiarity of the antique bottle is the uneven thickness of the glass. Often the base has a thick side that slopes to paper thinness on the opposite edge. This imperfection was eliminated with the introduction of the Owens bottle-making machine in 1903.

In addition, the various marks of stress and strain, sunken sides, twisted necks, and whittle marks (usually at the neck, where the wood mold made impressions in the glass) also give clues to indicate that a bottle was produced before 1900.

• LABELING AND EMBOSSING

While embossing and labeling were a common practice in the rest of the world for a number of centuries, large American bottle manufacturers with good financial backing began embossing with custom molds around 1810. Smaller, less lucrative companies did not begin embossing until about 1850. The inscriptions included information about the contents, manufacturer, distributor, slogans, or other messages advertising the product.

Manufacturers produced raised lettering using a plate mold, sometimes called a slug plate, fitted inside the casting mold. This plate created a sunken area and has resulted in these bottles being of a special value to collectors. Irregularities such as a misspelled name add to the value of the bottle, as will any name embossed with hand etching or other method of crude grinding. These bottles are very old, collectible, and valuable.

Inscription and embossing customs came to an end with the introduction of paper labels and the production of machine-made bottles beginning in 1903. In 1933, with the repeal of Prohibition, the distilling of whiskey and other spirits was resumed under new strict government regulations. One of the major regulations was that the following statement was required to be embossed on all bottles containing alcohol: "Federal Law Forbids Sale or Re-Use of this Bottle." This regulation was in effect until 1964 and is an excellent method of dating spirit bottles from 1933 to 1964.

Heinz food bottles: "Heinz's Evaporated Horse Radish," 6-1/2", **$125-$150**; "Heinz's Grape Jelly," 8", **$125-$150**; "Evaporated Horse Radish, H.J. Heinz Co.," 6-1/2", **$125-$150**, 1885-1920.

Determining Bottle Values

Collectors and dealers typically use rarity, age, condition, and color to determine bottle values. These factors are consistent with the criteria I have used over the years.

SUPPLY AND DEMAND

As with any product, when demand increases and supply decreases, prices increase.

CONDITION

Mint: An empty or full bottle (preferably full) with a label or embossing. The bottle must be clean and have good color, with no chips, scrapes, or wear. If the bottle comes in a box, the box must be in perfect condition, too.

Extra Fine: An empty or full bottle with slight wear on the label or embossing. The bottle must be clean with clear color, and no chips or scrapes. There is usually no box, or the box is not in very good condition.

Very Good: The bottle shows some wear, and the label is usually missing or not very visible. Most likely there is no embossing and no box.

Good: The bottle shows additional wear and the label is completely absent. The color is usually faded and the bottle is dirty and has some scrapes and minor chips. Most likely there is no box.

Fair or Average: The bottle shows considerable wear, the label is missing, and embossing is damaged.

RARITY

- **Unique:** A bottle is considered to be unique if only one is known to exist. These bottles are the most valuable and expensive.
- **Extremely Rare:** Only 5-10 known specimens.
- **Very Rare:** Only 10-20 known specimens.
- **Rare:** Only 20-40 known specimens.
- **Very Scarce:** No more than 50 bottles in existence.
- **Scarce:** No more that 100 bottles in existence.
- **Common:** Common bottles, such as clear 1880 to 1900 medicine bottles, are abundant, easy to acquire, usually very inexpensive, and great bottles for the beginning collector.

HISTORIC APPEAL, SIGNIFICANCE, AND GEOGRAPHY

For example: territorial bottles (bottles made in regions that had not yet been admitted to the Union) vs. bottles made in states admitted to the Union.

EMBOSSING, LABELING, AND DESIGN

Bottles without embossing are common and have little dollar value to many collectors. Exceptions are bottles handblown before 1840, which usually don't have embossing.

Embossing describes the name of the contents, manufacturer, state, city, dates, trademarks, and other valuable information. Embossed images and trademarks can also increase the value of the bottle.

Labeling found intact with all the specific information about the bottle also increases the value of the bottle.

AGE

While age can play an important role in the value of a bottle, there's not always a direct correlation. As stated in "The Beginning Collector" chapter, the history, rarity, and use of a bottle can be more important than age to a collector.

COLOR

- **Low Price:** clear, aqua, amber
- **Average Price:** milk glass, green, black, basic olive green
- **High Price:** teal blue, cobalt blue, purple (amethyst), yellow, yellow-green, puce

UNIQUE FEATURES

The following characteristics can also significantly affect value: pontil marks, whittle marks, glass imperfections (thickness and bubbles), slug plates, and crudely applied tops or lips.

Even with the above guidelines, it's important to consult more detailed references, especially concerning rare and valuable bottles. See the bibliography and the website listings at the back of this book. Remember, never miss a chance to ask other collectors and dealers for advice and assistance.

Bottle Sources

Antique and collectible bottles can be found in a variety of places and sometimes where you least expect them. The following provides a listing of abundant sources and potential hiding places for those much sought-after bottles, regardless if you are a beginning or veteran picker.

DIGGING FOR BOTTLES

Digging is a relatively inexpensive way to collect bottles and one heck of a lot of fun. While the "Digging for Bottles" section in this *Picker's Guide* (see P. 182) provides excellent detailed digging information, especially on privy or outhouse digging, the following information is an excerpt from that section on some specifics of where to find bottles.

Usually, settler and store owners hauled and dumped their garbage within one mile of the town limits. Or they would dig a hole about 25 yards from the back of their home or business for garbage and refuse. Many hotels and saloons had basements or underground storage areas where empty bottles were kept. Ravines, ditches, and washes are also prime digging spots because heavy rains or melting snow often washed debris down from other areas. Residents would store or throw their bottles under their porches when porches were common building features in the late 19th and 20th centuries, so bottles can often be found beside houses and under porches. Explore abandoned roads where houses or cabins once stood, wagon trails, old railroad tracks, and sewers. If it is legal, old battlegrounds and military encampments are excellent places to dig. Cisterns and wells are other good sources of bottles and period artifacts.

GHOST TOWNS

The first love of this bottle guy, and high on the list of many collectors, is an expedition to a ghost town. It's always fun and usually a great history lesson. The best places to search in ghost towns are near saloons, ravines and washes where miners dumped their trash, trade stores, abandoned buildings and shacks (look under the floors), old cellar and basements, the "red light" district, train stations, and the town dump (prior to 1900).

LAKES, RIVERS, AND OCEAN WATERS

Scuba diving for bottles has become popular in recent years. Just as settlers and store owners hauled their trash to dumps, many settlers, tavern owners, and trading post owners who lived near a waterway would pile their trash on a barge, take it out to the deepest part of the river or lake, and push the trash into the water. By doing this, they left behind great bottles that in many cases are rare or scarce and are in excellent condition. The ocean has always been a vast dumping ground of all sorts of trash, including bottles. Today there are many 17th and 18th century shipwrecks being found that are producing huge quantities of rare and scarce quality bottles. As more collectors become proficient in the skill of diving, the bottle-collecting world will see many more new quality finds from the past.

THE INTERNET AND SOCIAL MEDIA

In the 40 years that I've been collecting, I have never seen anything impact the hobby of bottle collecting as much as the Internet and social media sites. Search "Antique Bottle Collecting" and you'll be amazed at the amount of instant data immediately at your fingertips. Numerous websites throughout the United States, Canada, Europe, Asia, Central America, and Mexico provide detailed information about bottle clubs, dealers, sellers, antiques publications and books, auction companies, and eBay and other online auction sites. All of these Internet and social media sites have truly exposed bottle collecting to the entire world and have become convenient and inexpensive resource tools for all collectors.

FLEA MARKETS, SWAP MEETS, AND OTHER PLACES

For beginning collectors, these sources will likely be the most fun (next to digging) and yield the most bottles at the best prices. The majority of bottles found at these sources will fall into the common or common/above average category. You might find an occasional gem buried under the common stuff. The bottles are out there, you just need to look hard and long.

- **Flea markets, Swap Meets, and Thrift Stores**: Target areas where household goods are being sold. It's a good bet they will have bottles.
- **Garage Sales:** Focus on the older areas of town, since the items will be older, more collectible, and more likely to fall

into a rare or scarce category. Often these homes are up for sale through estate or probate sales and potentially can produce great finds.

- **Salvage Stores or Salvage Yards:** These are great places to search for bottles, since these businesses buy from companies that tear down old houses, apartments, and businesses. A New York salvage company discovered an untouched illegal Prohibition-era distillery complete with bottles, unused labels, and equipment. What a find!

LOCAL BOTTLE CLUBS AND COLLECTORS

By joining a local bottle club or working with collectors, you will find more ways to gather information, and do more digging. Members usually have quantities of unwanted or duplicate bottles, which they will sell very reasonably, trade, of sometimes even give away, especially to an enthusiastic newcomer. Quite often many of the club collectors are also dealers. If you make these collectors/dealers aware of what you are looking for, they will try to find it. Since most dealers usually have a varied number of contacts, it works to a picker's advantage to know as many dealers as possible.

BOTTLE SHOWS

Bottle shows not only expose collectors to bottles of every type, shape, color, and variety, but also provide them the opportunity to talk with experts in specialized fields. In addition, publications dealing with all aspects of bottle collecting are usually available for sale or even free. Bottle shows can be rewarding learning experiences not only for beginner collectors but also for veteran collectors. There are approximately 10 to 15 bottle shows across the country that take place almost every weekend, and they always offer something new to learn and share and, of course, bottles to buy or trade.

Make sure you look under the tables at these shows because many great bargains in the form of duplicates and unwanted items may be lurking there. Quite often, diggers find so many bottles they don't even bother to clean them. Instead, they put them under their tables and offer them as is for a very low price. Hey, for a low price I'll clean bottles!

AUCTIONS COMPANIES

Auction companies have become a great source of bottles and glassware over the last few years. A number of auctions house specialize only in bottles. When evaluating auction houses, look for companies that specialize in antiques and estate buyouts. To promote itself and provide buyers with a better idea of what will be presented for sale, an auction house usually publishes a catalog that can provide detailed bottle descriptions, conditions, and photographs. I recommend, however, that you first visit an auction as a spectator to learn how the process works before you decide to participate. When buying, be sure to check the color and condition of the bottle and terms of the sale. There are usually buyer and/or seller premiums in addition to the actual sale price. These guidelines also apply to all Internet auctions. Use caution and follow these general rules on P. 46. Note: If you are not sure about an item or what you are doing, ask someone in your club or another collector for advice.

Now that you've learned the abundant sources and potential hiding places for those much sought-after bottles, turn to P. 182 to learn what it takes to start your hunting adventures.

BUYING AT AUCTIONS

- Purchase the catalog and review all of the items in the auction. At live auctions, a preview is usually held for customers to inspect the items.
- After reviewing the catalog and making your choice, phone or mail your bid. A 10 percent to 20 percent buyer's premium is usually added to the sale price.
- Callbacks allow bidders to increase the previous high bid on certain items after the close of the auction.
- The winning bidder receives an invoice in the mail. After the bidder's check clears, the bottles are shipped.
- Most auction houses have a return policy, as well as a refund policy, for items that differ from the description in the catalog.

SELLING AT AUCTIONS

- Check and evaluate the auction source before consigning any merchandise. Make sure that the auction venue is legitimate and has not had any problems with payments or product.
- Package the item with plenty of bubble wrap, insure your bottle, and mail the package by certified mail, sign receipt requested.
- Allow 30 days to receive payment and be aware that most firms charge a fee of 15 percent commission on the sales price.

ESTATE SALES

An estate sale is a great source for bottles if the home is in an old neighborhood or section of the city with historical significance. These sales are a lot of fun, especially when the people running the sale let you look over and handle the items to be able to make careful selections. Prices are usually good and are always negotiable. In addition, always try to obtain the name of the company or person running the sale, and make sure to give them your name and number for information on future sales that may contain bottles.

KNIFE AND GUN SHOWS

Bottles at knife and gun shows? Yes. Quite a few gun and knife enthusiasts are also great fans of the West and keep an eye open for related artifacts. Every knife and gun show I've attended has had a number of dealers with bottles on their tables (or under the tables) for sale. And the prices were about right, since they were more interested in selling their knives and guns than the bottles. Plus, these dealers will often provide information on where they made their finds, which you can put to good use later.

RETAIL ANTIQUES DEALERS

This group includes dealers who sell bottles at or near full market prices. Buying from a dealer has advantages and disadvantages. They usually have a large selection and will provide helpful information and details about the bottles. And it's a safe bet that the bottles for sale are authentic. On the other hand, it can be very expensive to build a collection this way. But these shops are a good place to browse and learn.

GENERAL ANTIQUES AND SPECIALTY SHOPS

The difference between general and retail antiques shops is that general shops usually have lower prices and a more limited selection than retail shops. This is partly because merchants in general shops usually specialize in general collectible items and may not be as well informed about bottles. If a collector is well informed, general antiques dealers can provide the opportunity to acquire under-priced quality merchandise.

Bottle Handling

While selling bottles and listening to buyers at various shows, I am inevitably asked questions about cleaning, handling, and storing them. Some collectors believe that cleaning a bottle diminishes its collectible value and desirability. Leaving a bottle in its natural state, as it was found, can be special. Others prefer to remove as much dirt and residue as possible. The choice rests with the owner. The following information will provide some help with how to clean, store, and take care of those special finds.

BOTTLE CLEANING

First, never attempt to clean your new find in the field. In the excitement of the moment, it's easy to break the bottle or otherwise damage the embossing. With the exception of soda and ale bottles, glass bottles manufactured before 1875 usually have very thin walls. Even bottles with thicker walls should be handled very carefully.

The first step is to remove as much loose dirt, sand, or other particles as possible with a small hand brush or a soft-bristled toothbrush followed by a quick warm water rinse. Then, using a warm water solution and bleach (stir the mixture first), soak the bottles for a number of days (depending upon the amount of caked-on dirt). This should remove most of the excess grime. Also, adding some vinegar to warm water will add an extra sparkle to the glass. Other experienced collectors use cleaning mixtures such as straight ammonia, kerosene, Lime-A-Way, Mr. Clean, and chlorine borax bleach. Do not use mixtures that are not recommended for cleaning glass, never mix cleaners, and do not clean with acids of any type. Mixing cleaners has been known to release toxic gasses and poisonous vapors and fumes.

After soaking, the bottles may be cleaned with a bottle brush, steel wool, an old toothbrush, any semi-stiff brush, Q-tips, or used dental picks. At this point, you may want to soak the bottles again in lukewarm water to remove any traces of cleaning materials. Either let the bottles air-dry or dry them with a soft towel. If the bottle has a paper label, the work will be more painstaking since soaking is not a cleaning option. I've used a Q-tip to clean and dry the residue around the paper label.

Never clean your bottles in a dishwasher. While the hot water and detergent may produce a very clean bottle, these older bottles were not designed to withstand the extreme heat of a dishwasher. As a result, the extreme heat, along with the shaking, could crack or even shatter the bottles. In addition, bottles with any type of painted label may also be subjected to severe damage.

A better option is to consult a specialist who will clean your rare bottles with special tumbling, or cleaning machines. These machines work on the same principle as a rock tumbler with two parallel bars running horizontally acting as a "cradle" for the cleaning canisters. The key to the machine cleaning process is the two types of oxides that are used: polishing and cutting. The polishing oxides include aluminum, cerium, and tin, which remove stains and give the glass a crystal clean and polished appearance. The polishing oxides do not harm the embossing. The cutting oxides such as silicon carbide remove the etching and scratching. There are many individuals who are in the business of cleaning bottles with these machines, or you can also purchase the machines for personal use.

BOTTLE DISPLAY

Now that you have clean, beautiful bottles, display them to their best advantage. My advice is to arrange your bottles in a cabinet rather than on wall shelving or randomly around the house. While the last two options are more decorative, the bottles are more susceptible to damage. When choosing a cabinet, try to find one with glass sides that will provide more light and better viewing. As an added touch, a light fixture sets off a collection beautifully. If you still desire a wall shelving arrangement, make sure the shelf is approximately twelve inches wide, with a front lip for added protection. This can be accomplished with round molding. After the bottle is placed in its spot, draw an outline around the base of the bottle and then drill four 1/4-inch holes for pegs just outside the outline. The pegs will provide stability for the bottle. If you have picked up any other goodies from your digging, like coins or gambling chips, scatter them around the bottles for a Western flavor.

BOTTLE PROTECTION

Because of earthquakes, especially in northern and southern California, bottle collectors across the country have taken added steps to protect their valuable pieces.

Since most of us have our collections in some type of display cabinet, it's important to know how to best secure it. First, fasten the cabinet to the wall studs with brackets and bolts. If you are working with drywall and it's not possible to secure the cabinet to a stud, butterfly bolts will provide a tight hold. Always secure the cabinet at both the top and bottom for extra protection.

Next, lock or latch the cabinet doors. This will prevent the doors from flying open. If your cabinet has glass shelves, be sure to not overload them. In an earthquake, the glass shelving can break under the stress of excess weight.

Finally, it's important to secure the bottles to the shelves with materials such microcrystalline wax, beeswax, silicone adhesive, double-sided foam tape, adhesive-backed Velcro spots or strips. These materials are available at local home improvement centers and hardware stores. One of the newest and most commonly used adhesives is called Quake Hold. This substance, which is available in wax, putty, and gel, is similar to the wax product now used extensively by numerous museums to secure their artwork, sculptures, and various glass pieces. It is readily available to the general public at many home improvement stores and antique shops.

BOTTLE STORAGE

The best method for storing bottles you've chosen not to display is to place them in empty liquor boxes with cardboard dividers (which prevent bottles from knocking into each other). As added protection, wrap the individual bottles in paper prior to packing them in the boxes.

RECORDKEEPING

Last but not least, it's a good idea to keep records of your collection. Use index cards detailing where the bottle was found or purchased, including the dealer's name and price you paid. Assign a catalog number to each bottle, record it on the card, and then make an index. Many collectors keep records with the help of a photocopy machine. If the bottle has embossing or a label, put the bottle on the machine and make a copy of it. Another method is to make a pencil sketch by applying white paper to the bottle and rubbing over the embossing with a No. 2 pencil. Then, type all the pertinent information on the back of the image and put it in a binder. When it comes to trading and selling, excellent recordkeeping will prove to be invaluable.

Don't clean bottles in the field. Wait until you get home and can clean them carefully to avoid damaging them. *Courtesy of Rick Wiener.*

Barber bottle,
fiery opalescent
turquoise blue,
stars and stripes,
7", American
1885-1925,
$250-$350.

CHAPTER 1

Barber Bottles

Starting in the mid-1860s and continuing to 1920, barbers in America used colorful decorated bottles filled with various tonics and colognes. The finish of these unique and colorful pieces originated when the Pure Food and Drug Act of 1906 restricted the use of alcohol-based ingredients in unlabeled or refillable containers.

Very early examples will have rough pontil scars with numerous types of ornamentation such as fancy pressed designs, paintings, and labels under glass. The bottles were usually fitted with a cork, metal, or porcelain-type closure. Since the value of barber bottles is dependent upon the painted or enameled lettering or decoration, it is important to note that when determining the value of a barber bottle, any type of wear such as faded decoration or color, faded lettering, or chipping will lower its value.

Barber bottles, 8-1/2", opalescent milk glass, multicolored trumpet flower and vine decoration, "Witch Hazel" and "Bay Rum," smooth base, applied tops, American 1890-1915, **$200-$230.**

Barber bottle, 7-3/4", clear glass, enamel floral decoration on light blue frosted background, rib-pattern, pontil-scarred base, tooled top, American 1885-1920, **$250-$300.**

Barber bottle, 7-5/8", clear glass, bell shape, blue and white enamel decoration on pink frosted background, pontil-scarred base, tooled lip, American 1885-1920, **$180-$200.**

Barber bottle, 7-1/2", medium pink over white with fancy enameled decoration, pontiled base, tooled lip, American 1885-1920, **$100-$125.**

Barber bottle, 7-1/4", light turquoise blue, rib-pattern, ornate multicolored enamel floral design, polished pontil, tooled lip, American 1885-1920, **$200-$225.**

Barber bottle, 8-1/8", deep yellow green, rib-pattern, multicolored enamel floral decoration, pontil-scarred base, rolled lip, American 1885-1920, **$180-$225.**

Barber bottle, 10-1/2", turquoise blue with gold and white enamel, pontil base, tooled lip with original glass stopper, American 1885-1910, **$100-$125.**

Barber bottle, 6-7/8", fiery opalescent turquoise blue, swirl pattern, smooth base, rolled lip, American 1885-1920, **$100-$125.**

Barber bottle, 6-7/8", fiery opalescent turquoise blue, Spanish lace pattern, smooth base, rolled lip, American 1885-1920, **$100-$125.**

Barber bottle, 7", fiery opalescent clear glass, Stars & Stripes pattern, polished pontil, tooled top, American 1885-1920, **$200-$250.**

Barber bottle, 7-3/4", purple amethyst, rib-pattern, white enamel, grist mill decoration with words "Witch Hazel," smooth base, rolled lip, American 1885-1920, **$250-$300.**

Barber bottle, 8-1/8", medium emerald green, rib-pattern, white and orange enamel floral decoration, bell shape, pontil-scarred base, tooled top, American 1885-1920, **$200-$250.**

Barber bottle, 7-3/4", yellow green, rib-pattern, yellow and gold Art Nouveau style, floral decoration, pontil-scarred base, rolled lip, American 1885-1920, **$100-$125.**

Barber bottle, 8-7/8", deep powder blue milk glass, heavy enamel floral decoration with "Sea Foam," pontil-scarred base, rolled lip, American 1885-1920, **$90-$100.**

Barber bottle, 9", milk glass, multicolored floral decoration with "Hair Tonic," smooth base, rolled lip, American 1885-1920, **$140-$160.**

Barber bottle, 6-7/8", turquoise blue, rib-pattern, bell shape, orange, gold, and white enamel decoration, pontil-scarred base, tooled top, American 1885-1920, **$140-$180.**

Barber bottle, 7-3/4", medium cranberry, rib-pattern, blue and white enamel floral decoration, bell shape, pontil-scarred base, tooled top, American 1885-1920, **$200-$225.**

E.A. Olendorf /
Sarsaparilla Lager
(in slug plate) This
Bottle / Is Never
Sold, medium orange
amber, 9-1/4",
American 1885-
1895, **$250-$300**.

CHAPTER 2

Beer Bottles

Attempting to find an American beer bottle made before the mid-19th century is a difficult task. Until then, most bottles used for beer and spirits were imported. The majority of these imported bottles were black glass pontiled bottles made in three-piece molds and rarely embossed. There are four types of early beer bottles:

1. Porter, which is the most common: 1820 to 1920
2. Ale: 1845 to 1850
3. Early lager: 1847 to 1850 - rare
4. Late lager: 1850 to 1860

In spite of the large amounts of beer consumed in America before 1860, beer bottles were very rare and all have pontiled bases. Most beer manufactured during this time was distributed and dispensed from wooden barrels, or kegs, and sold to local taverns and private bottlers. Collectors often ask why various breweries did not bottle the beer they manufactured. During the Civil War, the federal government placed a special tax, levied by the barrel, on all brewed beverages. This taxing system prevented the brewery from making the beer and bottling it in the same building. Selling the beer to taverns and private bottlers was much simpler than erecting another building for bottling. This entire process changed after 1890 when the federal government revised the law to allow breweries to bottle beer straight from the beer lines.

Along with the brewing processes, the federal government also revised guidelines for bottle cleanliness.

The chart below reflects the age and rarity of beer bottles.

YEAR	RARE	SCARCE	SEMI-COMMON	COMMON
1860-1870	X			
1870-1880		X		
1880-1890			X	
1890-1930				X

Embossed bottles marked "Ale" or "Porter" were manufactured between 1850 and 1860. In the late 1860s, the breweries began to emboss their bottles with names and promotional messages. This practice continued into the 20th century. It is interesting to note that Pennsylvania breweries made most of the beer bottles from the second half of the 19th century. By 1890, beer was readily available in bottles around most of the country.

The first bottles used for beer in the United States were made of pottery, not glass. Glass did not become widely used until after the Civil War (1865). A wholesaler for Adolphus Busch named C. Conrad sold the original Budweiser beer from 1877 to 1890. The Budweiser name was a trademark of C. Conrad, but in 1891, it was sold to the Anheuser-Busch Brewing Association.

Before the 1870s, beer bottles were sealed with cork stoppers. Late in the 19th century, the lightning stopper was invented. It proved a convenient way of sealing and resealing blob top bottles. In 1891, corks were replaced with the crown cork closure invented by William Painter. This made use of a thin slice of cork within a tight-fitting metal cap. Once these were removed, they couldn't be used again.

Until the 1930s, beer came in green glass bottles. After Prohibition, brown glass came into use since it was thought to filter out damaging rays of the sun and preserve freshness.

Golden Gate Bottling Works – Chas. Roschmann – San Francisco – This Bottle Never Sold, light amber, one-half pint (split), tooled top, 1890-1910, **$300-$325.**

National Bottling Co. – San Francisco, Cal. – Adolph B. Lang, medium amber, quart, tooled top, 1910, **$60-$70.**

U.S. Bottling Co. – U.S. – Rapp & Debarry – S.F. Cal., medium amber, one-half pint (split), tooled top, 1893-1895, **$160-$180.**

Property Of – Chas. R. Puckhaber – Beers – Fresno, Cal., medium amber, one-half pint (split), crown tooled top, 1910-1920, **$125-$150.**

Gold Edge Bottling Works – J.F. Deininger – Vallejo, aqua, tooled top with original stopper, original wicker, 1890-1900, **$125-$150.**

Anheuser-Busch Brwg Assn. – Norfolk VA. Branch, aqua, pint, crown tooled top, 1910-1920, **$60-$70.**

Theodore Lutge & Co. – This Bottle Not To Be Sold – San Jose, Cal. Lime green, quart, applied top, 1885-1900, **$150-$175.**

Bay View – Brewing Co. – Seattle, Wash, mint green, quart, applied top, 1890-1905, **$200-$250.**

Assortment of five paper labeled beer bottles, two Old Nick (with contents), Cream City Brewery, Milwaukee – Pabst Sheboygan Aromatic Ginger Ale Beer – Pabst Breweries – Employees Beer – Milwaukee, Wisconsin – Jung's Pilsner Beer, 1920s-1930s, **$50 each.**

New England 'Stubby' Beer, 6-7/8", deep grass green (rare in this pure green color), iron pontil, applied double-collar top, blown in three-part mold, 1840-1860, **$100-$125.**

Saltglaze Stoneware Beer, 9-3/4", blob top, 'WC & J & G. Wilson/Sarsaparilla Mead" embossed at the top, American 1855-1870, **$100-1$25.**

Kensington – Brown Stout, 6-7/8", emerald green, iron pontil, applied top, American 1840-1860, **$240-$260.**

E. & G. Doughty Millville (in slug plate), Philadelphia XXX Porter &
Ale, 6-3/4", medium green, smooth base, applied double collar top,
American 1860-1870, **$375-$400.**

Dr. Cronk – R.MC.C, 10", 12-sided, cobalt blue, iron pontil, applied
tapered collar top, American 1850-1860, **$300-$325.**

J. Corwell (in slug plate) – Union Glass Works, Philada. Brown Stout, 6-3/4", sapphire blue, iron pontil, applied double collar top, American 1840-1860, **$1,000-$1,200.**

Dr. Bates Trade Mark National Tonic Beer Centennial 1876, This Bottle Never Sold, 8-5/8", red amber, smooth base, applied top, American 1876, **$275-$300.**

G.W. Hoxie's/ Premium/Beer, 6-3/4", rich blue green, smooth base, applied tapered collar top, American 1870-1885, **$275-$300.**

Property Of – Fredricksburg Brewery – San Jose Cal., red amber, quart, applied top, 1893-1906, **$250-$300.**

American Brewing Co. – West Berkley Cal. – This Bottle Not To Be Sold, medium amber, one-half pint (split), tooled top, 1890-1910, **$180-$200.**

Celebrated Nectar / Stomach Bitters / And Nerve Tonic – The / Nectar Bitter Co./ Toledo, O, bright yellow green, 9-3/8", American 1890-1900, **$275-$475.**

CHAPTER 3

Bitters Bottles

Bitters bottles have long been a favorite of bottle collectors. Because of their uniqueness, they were saved in great numbers, giving the collector great opportunities to build a special and varied collection.

Bitters, which originated in England, were a type of medicine made from bitter tasting roots or herbs, giving the concoction its name. During the 18th century, bitters were added to water, ale, or spirits with the intent to cure all types of ailments. Because of the pretense that those mixtures had some medicinal value, bitters became very popular in America since Colonists could import them from England without paying the liquor tax. While most bitters had low alcohol content, some brands ranged up as high as 120 proof, higher than most hard liquor available at the time. As physicians became convinced bitters had some type of healing value, the drink became socially acceptable, promoting use among people who normally weren't liquor drinkers.

The best known among the physicians who made their own bitters for patients was Dr. Jacob Hostetter. After his retirement in 1853, he gave permission to his son David to manufacture his "cure" commercially. Hostetter Bitters was known for its colorful, dramatic and extreme advertising. While Hostetter said it wouldn't cure everything, the list of ailments it claimed to alleviate with regular use covered most everything: indigestion, diarrhea, dysentery, chills and fever, liver ailments, and pains and weakness that came with old age (at that time, a euphemism for impotence). Despite these claims, David Hostetter died in 1888 from kidney failure, which should have been cured by his own bitters formula.

One of the most sought after bitters bottles and perhaps the most unique is Drakes Plantation Bitters that first appeared in 1860 and recorded a patent in 1862. The Drakes Bitters resembles the shape of a log cabin and can be found in four-log and six-log variations with colors in various shades of amber, yellow, citron, puce, green, and black. Another interesting characteristic of the Drake Bitters are the miscellaneous dots and marks including the "X" on the base of the bottles that are thought to be identification marks of the various glass houses that manufactured the bottles.

Most of the bitters bottles, over 1,000 types, were manufactured between 1860 and 1905. The more unique shapes called "Figurals" were in the likeness of cannons, drums, pigs, fish, and ears of corn. In addition to these shapes, others were round, square, rectangular, barreled-shaped, gin bottle-shaped, 12-sided, and flask-shaped. The embossed varieties are also the most collectible, oldest and most valuable.

The most common color was amber (pale golden yellow to dark amber brown), then aqua (light blue), and sometimes green or clear glass was used. The rarest and most collectible colors are dark blue, amethyst, milk glass and puce (a purplish brown).

Dr. A.W. Coleman's – Antidyspeptic and Tonic Bitters, dark blue green, 9-1/8", open pontil, applied tapered collar top, 1845-1860, **$850-$900**.

A.M.S.2 – 1864 – Constitution Bitters – A.M.S.2 – 1864 – Seward & Bentley – Buffalo, N.Y., medium olive amber, 9", smooth base, applied tapered collar top, 1865-1875, **$650-$700**.

Doctor Fisch's Bitters – W.H. Ware – Patented 1866, golden amber, figural fish, 11-1/2", smooth base, applied top, 1866-1875, **$250-$300**.

W & Co. – N.Y., yellow amber, 8-1/2", figural pineapple, open pontil, applied double collar top, 1855-1865, **$250-$275**.

Russ-St. Domingo Bitters –
New York, brilliant medium
olive green, 9-7/8", smooth
base, applied tapered
collar top, 1865-1875,
$5,500-$6,000.

Russ-St. Domingo Bitters
– New York, deep amber,
9-7/8", smooth base,
applied tapered collar top,
1865-1875, **$250-$350.**

Baker's
Orange Grove
Bitters,
9-1/2",
medium
amber,
smooth base,
applied
tapered
collar top,
American
1865-1875,
$650-$700.

Bourbon Whiskey Bitters,
9-1/2", medium cherry puce,
barrel shape, smooth base,
applied top, 1860-1870,
$400-$425.

William Allen's Congress Bitters,
deep blue aqua, 10-1/4",
semi-cabin shape, smooth
base, applied tapered collar top,
1865-1875, **$200-$225.**

American Stomach Bitters Co.
– Buffalo N.Y. – U.S.A., 11",
medium amber, cylinder shape,
smooth base, tooled top, 1885-
1895, **$800-$850.**

Figural barrel bitters bottle,
medium cobalt blue, 9-7/8",
smooth base, applied top, 1865-
1875, **$1,300-$1,500.**

Professor Geo. J. Byrne – New York – The Great Universal Compound – Stomach Bitters – Patented 1870-DC-CC-LX-XM-U.S.A, amber, 10-3/4", smooth base, applied tapered collar top, 1870-1875, **$1,600-$1,800.**

Brown's Celebrated Indian Herb Bitters – Patented – Feb 11 – 1868, clear glass with amethyst tone, 12-1/8", Indian queen, smooth base, sheared and ground lip, 1868-1875, **$20,000.**

The Great Tonic/Caldwell/Herb Bitters, 12-5/8', amber, iron pontil, applied tapered collar top, American 1865-1870, **$125-$135.**

Brown & Lyon's Blood Bitters – Binghamton, N.Y., medium golden yellow amber, 9-7/8", smooth base, applied tapered collar top, 1870-1880, **$300-$350.**

Botanic/(Motiff of Sphinx) Bitters-Herzberg Bros-New York, 9-3/4", golden yellow amber, smooth base, applied tapered double collar top, American 1875-1880, **$600-$700.**

Bourbon Whiskey Bitters, 9-3/8", medium smoky gray topaz, barrel shape, smooth base, applied top, American 1860-1870, **$3,700-$3,900.**

Buhrer's Gentian Biters – S.Buhrer Proprietor, 9", orange amber, smooth base, applied top, American 1870-1880, **$125-$135.**

Argyle Bitters/E.B Wheelock/N.O., deep olive green, 9-1/2", rare bottle in rare color, smooth base, applied top, American 1870-1880, **$2,700-$3,000.**

Dr. Flint's – Quaker Bitters, 9-1/2", Aqua, smooth base, applied top, original unopened wrapper, label, and contents, label reads: 'Dr. Flint's Quaker Bitters, Prepared by Cross & Clarke, at there Great Medical Depot, Lawrence, Mass.', American 1885-1895, **$550-$600.**

Brown's Celebrated Indian Herb Bitters-Patented Feb. 11, 1868, 12-1/4", yellow amber, Indian Princess, smooth base, sheared and inward rolled lip, American 1868-1875, **$400-$425.**

Dr. A. S. Hopkins Union Stomach Bitters F.S. Amidon, Sole Prop. Hartford, Conn. U.S.A., 9-1/2", medium amber, smooth base, tooled top, original back and front labels, American 1890-1910, **$700-$800.**

Horse Shoe Bitters-Horse Shoe Medicine Co (motif of running horse) Collinsville Ills, 8-5/8', medium amber shading to yellow amber, figural horseshoe on side, smooth base, tooled top, American 1890-1900, **$3,200-$3,400.**

Black glass presentation stippled wine bottle, "A Present – From – George Aitken – to George Cairns – of Arme Cairns Aitken (thistle alongside a coat-of-arms) – 'Efflo Eseo' (large cornucopia)," dark olive amber, 10-1/4", Scotland 1835-1860, **$550-$600**.

CHAPTER 4

Black Glass

Whenever I see or handle black glass bottles at various shows or view displays, I immediately think of the shipwrecks of English whaling and cargo ships and Spanish galleons lying of the bottom of the Atlantic, Pacific, and East-Indian oceans. The good news for the collectors is that not all of these ships went down, and the sailors and merchants who made dry land left behind plenty of black glass bottles. These bottles were actually the first glass containers with liquid contents shipped to America from Holland, England, Germany, Belgium, France, Italy, Spain and other European countries from the early 16th to the mid-19th centuries.

Until the mid-1800s, trade merchants believed that dark glass containers would provide a method of preserving their products for the long ship voyages and lengthy storage, resulting in an increased demand for black glass bottles. This demand caused the glasshouses to increase production and quickly produce an inexpensive type of black glass. By adding iron slag to the basic glass mixture of sand, soda and lime, they were able to produce the desired black glass. As the glass continued to be developed and improved, black glass proved to be durable and withstand more exposure to the natural elements as well as the shipping and handling process during the rough sea voyages and treacherous land trips. Another interesting fact is that not all black glass is actually black, but dark olive green. If you hold up a black glass bottle to good lighting, you will be able to observe the olive green tint.

The black glass bottles were manufactured by the free-blown method and therefore it's difficult to find any two bottles that are alike in shape. As the usage expanded, the bottles evolved into various shapes, forms, styles and sizes.

CATEGORY	1630-1680	1650-1840	1690-1720	1725-1780	1760-1850	1780-1840
Shaft & Globe	X					
Seal Bottles		X				
Onion Squat			X			
Mallet				X		
Cylindrical Bottles					X	
Utility & Other Bottles						X

SHAFTS & GLOBES

The shaft and globe bottles made before 1630 were very fragile due to the early glass process and wood resource problems, and didn't last long during any type of travel. Therefore, not many of these bottles survived. It wasn't until the 1630s-1650s when the English glasshouses improved the development of their processes by burning coal instead of wood, and developed additional techniques to improve bottle making resulting in a more durable and longer lasting bottle.

SEAL BOTTLES

The process of attaching glass seals to the shoulder or bodies of wine bottles started in the mid-1600s in England. The method for this process was to apply the seal after the bottle was completed but not cooled (annealed). Then a glob of glass was taken from the furnace and fused to the still hot bottle. While the glob was still hot it was impressed with a stamp, similar to a stamp being impressed into sealing wax. These stamps would have the letters or design of the owners of the bottles. In some cases, the seals also included the date the bottle was manufactured or initially used, which can be helpful for dating the bottles.

ONION SQUAT BOTTLES

Squat wine bottles were manufactured in England from around 1600-1830 while the Dutch also made squat wine bottles during the 17th century. Some of the differences between the English and Dutch bottles:

- The Dutch version usually has a longer neck than the English model.
- English bottles have a non-existent base kick-up and a small pontil scar.
- Dutch bottles have a severe base kick-up and a large pontil scar.
- The Dutch bottleneck features a flat wraparound rim.
- English bottlenecks have an applied collar (laid-on ring).

MALLET BOTTLES

As the demand from merchants increased for longer-term storage of wine, the onion squat bottles changed their shape around 1720 to be manufactured in a flatter shape resembling a mallet (tool). By the 1730s, the tapered shape started losing favor and the mallet bottles were manufactured with slight tapers, with narrower and deeper bodies with longer necks. By 1740 mallets were manufactured with longer necks, and by 1750 the neck length was becoming less than the body height.

CYLINDRICAL BOTTLES

The earliest shapes of cylinder bottles were introduced around 1760 with the now standard wide body increasing in height and decreasing in width. In terms of storage and space, merchants were pleased with the thinner cylinder bottles rather than the mallet or squat-shaped bottles. By 1780, cylinder bottles were becoming more popular, and between 1820-1850, with the perfection of three-piece molds and other methods, the majority of wine bottles were being manufactured in the shape.

UTILITY AND OTHER BOTTLES

Utility bottles are exactly what the name implies. These bottles were usually blown with a wide top or mouth and were used to store food supplies, snuff, ink, rum, gin, whiskey, or anything else that required a container for storage. These bottles, made by the thousands and often used and reused because of their durability, can be found in a wide variety of shapes and sizes.

Black glass magnum shape wine bottle (id seal "21"), "PS" script letters, dark olive green, 12-1/4", English or American 1790-1810, **$850-$900.**

Black glass triangular wine bottle (Masonic seal), deep olive amber, 9-3/8", Scotland 1845-1860, very rare, **$2,300-$2,500.**

Black glass pancake onion or ship bottle, dark amber, 9-1/4", 7-1/4" diameter, Scotland 1820-1840, **$550-$650.**

Black glass globular bottle with hand stippled decoration, 8-5/8",
dark olive amber, pontil-scarred base, applied double collar top,
Scotland, 1870, **$400-$500.**

Black glass mallets, olive
amber, 7-5/8" and 7-7/8'
English 1735-1755,
$125-$150.

Black glass onion shape
wine bottle, medium olive
green, 6-7/8" x 5-1/2"
diameter, Dutch 1720-
1750, **$250-$300.**

Black glass globular bottle, Andrew Dobble, 8-1/2", dark olive amber, pontil-scarred base, applied double collar top, Scotland 1837, **$500-$600.**

Onion-shaped wine bottle, or storage bottle, 9-1/4", yellow olive amber, open pontil, sheared lip with an applied top, Dutch, 1770-1790, **$350-$400.**

Black glass onion, deep yellow green, 7-1/8" x 5-3/8"diameter, Dutch 1820-1840, **$150-$200.**

Magnum wine bottle – Perkins (on applied seal), 12", dark olive amber, pontil-scarred base, applied double collar top and seal, blown in a dip mold, English, 1790-1820, **$800-$900.**

Black glass wine bottle, 7-5/8", deep olive green, pontil-scarred base, sheared top with applied string lip, blown in dip mold, English, 1770-1780, **$150-$170.**

Fire grenade, "Spong & Cos Hand Fire Extinguishing Tube & Grenade – London," yellow olive, 12-3/4" long, tooled lip, English 1880-1900, **$400-$475.**

CHAPTER 5

Fire Grenades

Fire grenades are a highly prized item among bottle collectors and represent one of the first modern improvements in fire fighting. A fire grenade is a water-filled bottle about the size of a baseball. Its use was simple. It was designed to be thrown into a fire, where it would break and (hopefully) extinguish the flames. The fire grenades worked best when the fire was noticed immediately.

The first American patent on a fire grenade was issued in 1863 to Alanson Crane of Fortress Monroe, Virginia. The best-known manufacturer of these specialized bottles, the Halden Fire Extinguisher Co., Chicago, Illinois, was awarded a patent in August of 1871.

The grenades were manufactured in large numbers by companies with names as unique as the bottles themselves: Dash-Out, Diamond, Harkness Fire Destroyer, Hazelton's High Pressure Chemical Firekeg, Magic Fire, Y-Burn, Hayward Hand Grenade.

The fire grenade became obsolete with the invention of the fire extinguisher in 1905. Many of these grenades are considered rare and scarce and can still be found with the original closures, contents, and labels.

Fire grenade, "Hazelton's High Pressure Chemical Fire Keg," amber, 11", tooled lip, original metal neck band and swing handle, American 1875-1896, **$450-$500.**

Fire grenade, "L'Incombustibilite – Paris," orange amber, 5-3/8", sheared and ground lip, French 1880-1900, $100-$125.

Fire Keg – Hazelton's High Pressure Chemical Fire Keg, 11-1/8", medium amber, smooth base, tooled top, original metal neck band and loop handle, American 1880-1900, $450-$500.

Fire grenade, medium sapphire blue, original red label with gold lettering reads "Fire Destroyer," original contents and wire hanger, 6-1/8", American 1875-1895, **$500-$600.**

Fire grenade, "Barnum's Hand Fire – Ext. Diamond Pat.d – June 26th – 1869 – Diamond," 6-1/8", rough sheared lip, American 1870-1895, **$100-$125.**

Fire grenade, unembossed with horizontal rib-pattern, deep cobalt blue, 6-1/8", ground lip, American 1875-1895, **$275-$300.**

Fire grenade, "Hayward's Hand Fire Grenade – S.F. Hayward – 407 Broadway – N.Y. – Patented Aug. – 8 – 1871," golden yellow amber, 6-1/8" tooled lip, American 1873-1895, **$200-$225.**

Fire grenade, "Rockford –Kalamazoo – Automatic And – Hand Fire Extinguisher – Patent applied For," cobalt blue, 11", tooled lip, American 1875-1895, **$500-$600.**

Fire grenade, "Magic – Fire – Extinguisher Co.," golden yellow amber, 6-1/4", sheared and ground lip, American 1875-1895, **$600-$700.**

Fire grenade, "Prevoyante – Extincteur – Grenade," orange amber, 5-5/8", sheared and ground lip, French 1875-1895, **$100-$125.**

Fire grenade, "Hayward's Hand Fire Grenade – S.F. Hayward – 407 Broadway- N.Y. – Patented Aug. – 8 –1871," medium turquoise blue, 6-3/8" tooled lip, American 1871-1895, **$300-$325.**

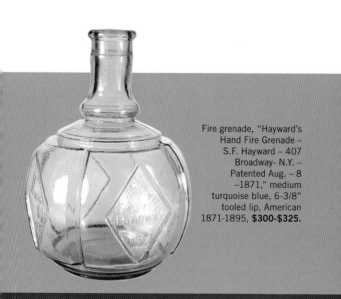

Fire grenade, "Hayward's Hand Fire Grenade – S.F. Hayward – 407 Broadway- N.Y. – Patented Aug. – 8 –1871," medium lime green, 6-1/8", sheared and tooled lip, American 1872-1895, **$200-$250.**

Fire grenade, "Hayward's Hand Fire Grenade – S.F. Hayward – 407 Broadway- N.Y. – Patented Aug. – 8 –1871," olive yellow, 6-1/8", sheared and tooled lip, original neck foil, content, label, American 1872-1895, **$300-$350.**

Fire grenade, "Hayward's Hand Fire Grenade- S.F. Hayward-407 Broadway – N.Y. – Patented Aug.-8 – 1871", Deep Cobalt Blue, tooled lip, American 1873-1895, **$200-$225.**

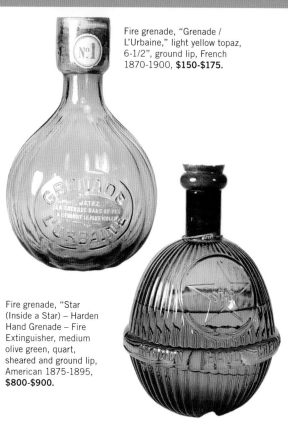

Fire grenade, "Grenade / L'Urbaine," light yellow topaz, 6-1/2", ground lip, French 1870-1900, **$150-$175.**

Fire grenade, "Star (Inside a Star) – Harden Hand Grenade – Fire Extinguisher, medium olive green, quart, sheared and ground lip, American 1875-1895, **$800-$900.**

Fire grenade, "Grenade Labbe-Grenade-Labbe-L'Incombustibilite 139 Rue La Fayette-Paris," orange amber, 5-1/2", sheared and ground lip, French 1880-1900, **$125-$150.**

This extremely rare history flask, a cobalt blue "Washington Bust – Tree in Leaf" portrait flask (GI-35), 1845-1860, sold at auction for **$24,000.**

Norm Heckler Auctions

CHAPTER 6

Flasks

Flasks have become a most popular and prized item among collectors due to the variety of decorative, historical, and pictorial depictions on many pieces. The outstanding colors have a major effect on the value of these pieces, more so than most other collectible bottles.

American flasks were first manufactured by the Pitkin Glasshouse in Connecticut around 1815, and quickly spread to other glass houses around the country. Early flasks were free-blown and represent some of the better craftsmanship with more intricate designs. By 1850, approximately 400 designs had been used. Black graphite pontil marks were left on the bottles because the pontils were coated with powdered iron allowing the flasks' bottoms to break away without damaging the glass. The flasks made between 1850 and 1870, however, had no such markings because of the widespread use of the newly invented snap-case.

Since flasks were intended to be refilled with whiskey or other spirits, more time and effort were expended in manufacturing than most other types of bottles. Flasks soon became a popular item for use with all types of causes and promotions. Mottos frequently were embossed

Johnson & Burke – Turf Exchange – 114 Main St. – Anaconda Mont., clear glass, half-pint, tooled top, American 1885-1895, **$700-$800.**

on flasks and included a number of patriotic sayings and slogans. George Washington's face commonly appeared on flasks, as did Andrew Jackson's and John Quincy Adams, the candidates for the presidential elections of 1824 and 1828. Events of the time were also portrayed on flasks.

One of the more controversial flasks was the Masonic flask, which bore the order's emblem on one side and the American eagle on the other side. At first, the design drew strong opposition from the public, but the controversy soon passed, and Masonic flasks are now a specialty items for collectors.

Another highly collectible flask is the Pitkin-type flask named for the Pitkin Glassworks, where it was exclusively manufactured. While Pitkin-type flasks and ink bottles are common, Pitkin bottles, jugs, and jars are rare. German Pitkin flasks are heavier and straight-ribbed, while the American patterns are swirled and broken-ribbed with unusual colors such as dark blue.

Because flasks were widely used for promoting various political and special interest agendas, they represent a major historical record of the people and events of those times.

Boitano's – Special – Straight – Whiskey – Sacramento, Cal., (label), clear glass, pint pumpkin seed, American 1885-1895, **$100-$125.**

The Peerless – A. Fuhrberg - Prop – Anaheim, Calif., clear glass, pint, tooled top, American 1890-1915, **$250-$350.**

Louisville Liquor House – 306 Bennett Ave. – Cripple Creek, Col., clear glass, half-pint, tooled top, American 1890-1910, **$500-$600.**

G.E. Crowley Wine Merchant –18 South Main St. – Butte, Mont., clear glass, half-pint, tooled top, American 1885-1895, **$450-$500.**

Two strapside whiskey flasks, "John Coyne – Cor. Fayette & Seneca Sts. – Utica, N.Y.," yellow green, pint, applied top, and "D.F. Flagg & Co. – 165 Blackstone St – Boston," tooled double collar top, American 1880-1900, **$250-$300.**

Fleckenstein & Mayer FM Co. (Monogram) Portland, Oregon, pint, 7-1/2", reddish amber, smooth base, drippy double applied collar top, American 1877-1885, **$600-$700.**

H. Brickwedel & Co. / Wholesale/Liquor Dealers / 208 & 210/ Front St./S.F., Pint, 7-3/8", Orange Amber, smooth base, tooled single collar top, American 1880-1883, **$325-$350.**

(Glass Works Auction–CD 101-Lot No. 9)

Eagle – Louisville KY Glass Works, half pint, amber, smooth base, applied double collar top, American 1855-1860, **$700-$800.**

Kossuth with bust of Kossuth – Tree, medium grass green calabash, Pontil-scarred base, applied tapered collar top, American 1855-1865, **$350-$400** rare color.

Liberty with oak tree – Eagle, half pint, amber, open pontil, sheared and tooled top, American 1825-1835, **$1,400-$1,500.**

J.N. Kline & CO's, Aromatic Digestive Corial (All inside an embossed wreath), 5-3/8", medium cobalt blue, smooth base, applied double collar top, American 1860-1870, **$425-$500.**

Label under glass whiskey flask, clear pocket flask with American soldier and sailor shaking hands, 5-7/8", smooth base, sheared and ground lip, original metal screw cap and shot glass, American 1898-1900, (commemorative flask Spanish American War) **$1,000-$1,200.**

Trade Mark / Lighting, medium yellow green, quart, American 1875-1890, **$275-$375**.

CHAPTER 7

Fruit Jars

Fruit jars were sold empty for use in home preservation of many different types of food. They were predominant in the 1800s when pre-packaged foods weren't available and home canning was the only option. Although fruit jars carry no advertising, they aren't necessarily common or plain since the bottle manufacturer's name is usually embossed in large lettering along with the patent date. The manufacturer whose advertising campaign gave fruit jars their name was Thomas W. Dyott, who was in the market early selling fruit jars by 1829.

For the first 50 years, the most common closure was a cork sealed with wax. In 1855, an inverted saucer-like lid was invented that could be inserted into the jar to provide an air tight seal. The Hero Glassworks invented the glass lid in 1856 and improved upon it in 1858 with a zinc lid invented by John Landis Mason, who also produced fruit jars. Because the medical profession warned that zinc could be harmful, Hero Glassworks developed a glass lid for the Mason jar in 1868. Mason eventually transferred his patent rights to the Consolidated Fruit Jar Co., which let the patent expire.

In 1880, the Ball Brothers began distributing Mason jars, and in 1898 the use of a semi-automatic bottle machine increased the output of the Mason jar until the automatic machine was invented in 1903.

Fruit jars come in a wide variety of sizes and colors, but the most common are aqua and clear. The rarer jars were made in various shades of blue, amber, black, milk glass, green and purple.

Franklin – Fruit Jar, aqua, quart, ground lip, American 1865-1875, **$250-$350.**

A. Stone & Co. – Philada, aqua, quart, pressed down groove wax sealer, American 1860-1870, **$250-$300.**

Sure, aqua, quart, ground lip, original glass lid and wire closure, American 1870-1880, **$600-$700.**

R.M. Dalbey's Fruit Jar, Pat Nov 10 1858, quart, blue aqua, smooth base, sheared and ground top, original metal lid, three thumbscrews and metal neck ring, American 1860-1865, **$9,000–$10,000.**

Whitmore's – Patent – Rochester – N.Y., aqua, half-gallon, ground lip, American 1868-1875, **$100-$125.**

C. Burnham & Co. – Manufacturers – Philada, apple green, quart, ground lip, American 1860-1870, **$900-$1,000.**

Belle, aqua, quart, sheared and ground lip, original domed glass lid, American 1869-1875, **$1,200-$1,300.**

Joshua Wright – Philada, pale aqua, 10-5/8", iron pontil, rolled lip, American 1845-1860, **$350-$375.**

Fridley & Cornman's – Patent – Oct. 25th 1859 – Ladies Choice, deep blue aqua, quart, ground lip, original iron closure, American 1859-1865, **$1,800-$2,000.**

Mansfield – Glass Works
– Sole MFR's, clear glass,
quart, American 1910-1915,
$700-$750.

Safety – Wide Mouth – Mason
– Salem Glass Works – Salem,
N.J., blue aqua, quart, original
metal beater, American 1915-
1925, **$850-$900.**

Mason's (Keystone) – Patent –
Nov 30th – 1858, yellow amber,
pint, ground lip, American 1875-
1895, **$1,200-$1,400.**

Pacific – S.F. – Glassworks
– Victory Jar, aqua green,
quart, original closure,
American 1870-1880,
$300-$350.

Hollister
Drug Co. LD.
– Honolulu,
early 1900s,
$700-$900.

CHAPTER 8

Hawaiian Bottles

The history, culture, and beauty of the Hawaiian Islands are intertwined with the history of the many varieties of bottles from the islands. While Hawaii, sometimes referred to as "The Aloha State," didn't become a U.S. state until 1959, its history and culture began centuries earlier, when a 1,600-mile-long fissure on the floor of the Pacific Ocean produced the Hawaiian Ridge.

Along the top of this ridge were individual protrusions of domes that over time formed the Hawaiian Islands: Hawaii (The Big Island), Maui, Oahu, Kauai, Molokai, and Lanai. Approximately 1,500 years ago, Polynesians from the South Pacific found the Hawaiian Islands. About 500 years later, settlers from Tahiti arrived and initiated a ruling king for each island. Social classes emerged, and the Hawaiian culture began to form.

Captain James Cook founded Oahu and Kauai on Jan. 18, 1778. He named Hawaii the Sandwich Islands in honor of the Earl of Sandwich, but he met his demise in a battle with natives on Feb. 13, 1779. In 1810, King Kamehameha I unified the Hawaiian Islands under a single rule and soon promoted trade with Europe and the United States. Hawaiian rule continued until 1893, but Western influence continued to grow, and American colonists overthrew the Hawaiian kingdom on Jan. 17, 1893. In 1898, Hawaii officially became a territory of the United States.

BOTTLING COMPANIES, MANUFACTURERS, AND DATING OF BOTTLES

The timeline of Hawaii's history directly relates to the extensive importing of bottles dating back to 1851, when German merchant Ulrich Alting imported the first known Hawaiian embossed soda bottles. As the need intensified to satisfy the numerous ships arriving in Honolulu carrying whalers, sailors, English visitors, and settlers, the need to satisfy their thirst also increased. In addition to the Alting imports, C. L. Richards & Co. began importing embossed whiskey bottles around 1878, and Geo. C. McLean started importing blob top blown sodas around 1885.

The continued influx of visitors and new inhabitants eventually led to the establishment of Hawaii's first bottling companies in the early 1880s, and when Hawaii became a territory of the United States in 1898, many more bottling companies came into existence.

While the islands have produced a variety of bottles, the most common and numerous were the soda bottles that have become the highlight of most Hawaiian bottle collections. As an example, when pineapple companies became the main economy of Hawaii,

Hawaiian Soda Works – Honolulu, H.I., 1899, **$1,700-$4,600.**

each island had its own sugar and pineapple company with its own company store. During the late 1880s into the early 1900s, there were more than 44 different soda companies that manufactured Hutchinson, crown top, and over 270 variations of BIMALS (bottles hand blown into a mold) soda bottles. These many variations rank right at the top of the majority of Hawaiian bottle collections.

During the most productive years, Hawaii's four largest and most populated islands, Oahu, Kauai, Maui, and the Big Island, shared these 44 bottling companies, with 25 of them located on Oahu. Besides the manufacturing of soda, products also included whiskey, gin, beer, medicines, and milk.

Sailors and whalers who drank their whiskey in Hawaii prior to 1898 drank from bottles manufactured for Hawaiian companies that were embossed H.I. (Hawaiian Islands) or in some cases S.I. (Sandwich Islands), which can be found on whiskey bottles dating to the late 1850s. After Hawaii became a U.S. Territory in 1898, the abbreviation H.T. (Hawaiian Territory) or T.H. (Territory of Hawaii) appeared on the bottles and was carried through statehood in 1959. The use of the initials H.I. and H.T. continued on Hawaiian BIMALS and machine-made bottles well into the 1920s and early 1930s.

Property of Hawaiian Soda Works – Honolulu T.H., 1910, **$550-$750.**

Property of Hawaiian –
Soda Works – Honolulu.
T.H., 1910, **$500-$900.**

Registered – This Bottle Is
The Property Of – Arctic Soda
Water Works – Honolulu, T.H.,
1910, **$400-$600.**

Hollister & Co.,
Honolulu, 1870s,
$175-$250.

Tahiti – Lemonade
– Works Company
– Honolulu. H.,
1892, **$300-$400.**

Hanapepe – Soda Works – Hanapepe – Kauai, 1905, **$400-$600.**

Macfarlane & Co. (monogram "M"), Honolulu, 1910, **$175-$225.**

Pacific – Soda Works – Hilo, Hawaii, 1910, **$400-$600.**

Hollister Drug Co. Ld – Honolulu, mid-1890s, **$150-$200.**

Hollister Drug Co.
(monogram "HD")
– Honolulu, 1905,
$250-$400.

Hilo Drug Co.
Limited – Hilo,
Hawaii, 1905,
$250-$400.

Property Of – One Quart – EWA – Plantation – Dairy, 1925-1930, **$400-$700.**

New Pacific Dairy – Phone 850A – Paiahhloa, 1940-1950, **$700-$800.**

Birmingham – Coca-
Cola Bottling Co.,
clear, 7", American
1885-1900,
$1,800-$2,200.

CHAPTER 9

Hutchinson Bottles

Charles A. Hutchinson developed the Hutchinson bottle in the late 1870s. Interestingly, the stopper, not the bottle itself, differentiated the design from others. The stopper, which Hutchinson patented in 1879, was intended as an improvement over cork stoppers, which eventually shrank and allowed the air to seep into the bottle.

The new stopper consisted of a rubber disc that was held between two metal plates attached to a spring stem. The stem was shaped like a figure eight, with the upper loop larger than the lower to prevent the stem from falling into the bottle. The lower loop could pass through the bottle's neck and push down the disc to permit the filling or pouring of it contents. A refilled bottle was sealed by pulling the disc up to the bottles shoulder, where it made a tight fit. When opened, the spring made a popping sound. Thus, the Hutchinson bottle had the honor of originating the phrase "pop bottle," which is how soda came to be known as "pop."

Hutchinson stopped producing bottles in 1912, when warnings about metal poisoning were issued. As collectibles, Hutchinson bottles rank high on the curiosity and price scales, but pricing varies quite sharply by geographical location, compared to the relatively stable prices of most other bottles.

Hutchinson bottles carry abbreviations of which the following three are the most common:
- TBNTBS - This bottle not to be sold
- TBMBR - This bottle must be returned
- TBINS - This bottle is not sold

Phil Daniels – Anaconda – Mont., aqua green, 6-3/4", tooled top, American 1885-1895, **$150-$200.**

Anaconda – Bottling Co. – Anaconda, Mont., clear, 7", tooled top, American 1885-1895, **$125-$150.**

Bozeman – Bottling Co. – Bozeman, Mont., medium green, 7", tooled top, American 1885-1895, **$250-$275.**

City Ice – Bottling Wks – Georgetown – Texas, bright green, 7-1/8", American 1895-1905, **$400-$425.**

Claus Brothers – Birch Beer – Elizabeth – NJ – This Bottle/ Not To Be Sold, 7-1/4", light to medium yellow green, smooth base, tooled top, American 1890-1910, **$300-$400.**

Benica – Steam-Soda Works – Custav Gnauch, medium green, 7", American 1901-1915 (rare), **$125-$150.**

Guilbert – Yreka, medium green, 7", tooled top, American 1885-1895, **$125-$150**.

J. F. Deegan – Pottsville – PA, medium yellow amber, 6-3/4", tooled top, American 1885-1895, **$450-$475.**

Pittsburgh Bottling – J & D Miller – House, medium cobalt blue, 7-1/8", tooled top, American 1885-1900, **$350-$400.**

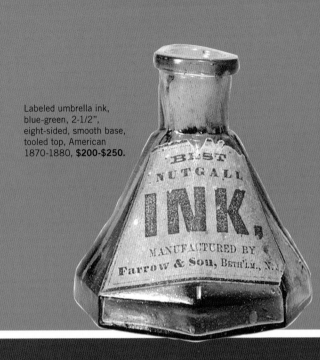

Labeled umbrella ink, blue-green, 2-1/2", eight-sided, smooth base, tooled top, American 1870-1880, **$200-$250.**

Labeled umbrella ink, medium blue green, 2-3/8", eight-sided, open pontil, rolled lip, American 1840-1860, **$125-$150.**

CHAPTER 10

Ink Bottles

Ink bottles are unique because of their centuries-old history, which provides collectors today with a wider variety of designs and shapes than any other group of bottles. People often ask why a product as cheap to produce as ink was sold in such decorative bottles. While other bottles were disposed of or returned after use, ink bottles were usually displayed openly on desks in dens, libraries, and studies. It's safe to assume that even into the late 1880s people who bought ink bottles considered the design of the bottle as well as the quality of its contents.

Prior to the 18th century, most ink was sold in brass or copper containers. The rich would then refill their gold and silver inkwells from these storage containers. Ink that was sold in glass and pottery bottles in England in the 1700s had no brand name identification, and, at best, would have a label identifying the ink and/or the manufacturer.

In 1792, the first patent for the commercial production of ink was issued in England, 24 years before the first American patent that was issued in 1816. Molded ink bottles began to appear in America around 1815-1816 and the blown three-mold variety came into use during the late 1840s. The most common shaped ink bottle, the umbrella, is a multi-sided conical that can be found with both pontiled and smooth bases. One of the more collectible ink bottles is the teakettle, identified by the neck, which extends upward at an angle from the base.

As the fountain pen grew in popularity between 1885-1890, ink bottles gradually were less decorative and became just another plain bottle.

Cone inkwell, emerald green, 2-1/2", pontil base, rolled lip, American 1850-1855, **$350-$400.**

Labeled umbrella ink, medium amber, eight-sided, smooth base, tooled top, 2-5/8", American 1870-1880, **$100-$130.**

First Premium
STEEL PEN
INK
PREPARED BY
THADDEUS DAVIDS &CO
WARRANTED Nº 127 & 129 William

Cone ink, deep olive green, 2-3/8", open pontil, tooled lip,
American 1840-1860, **$500-$550.**

A.M. Bertinguiot, cobalt blue, 2-3/8", open pontil, inward rolled lip,
American 1840-1860, **$650-$700.**

Harrison's Columbian Ink, cobalt blue, 5-3/4", open pontil, applied top, American 1840-1860, **$700-$750.**

Saltglazed stoneware bulk ink jug, "A-W Harrison Patent Columbian Ink Philadelphia," 9-7/8", handled, American 1850-1860, **$900-$1,000.**

Labeled umbrella ink, medium blue-green, 2-1/2", eight-sided, pontil-scarred base, rolled lip, American 1840-1860, **$350-$375.**

Master Ink – E. Waters Troy, NY, 6-7/8", aqua, open pontil, applied top, 16-fluted shoulder panels, American 1840-1860, **$650-$750.**

Umbrella Ink, 2-1/4", 6-sided with indented label panel, yellow olive green, open pontil, tooled top, American 1840-1860, **$2,000-$2,100.**

Umbrella Ink, 2-1/4", 8-sided, medium cobalt blue, open pontil, inward rolled lip, American 1840-1860, $**1,300-$1,400.**

Cone Ink – Wood's Black Ink/ Portland, 2-3/8", yellow amber, open pontil, sheared and tooled lip, American 1840-1860, **$700-$800**.

Umbrella ink, Davis & Miller, blue aqua, 2-1/2", open pontil, American 1840-1860, **$400-$425**.

FINE BLACK INK
Sold Wholesale & Retail
BY H. K. LOGAN
S. W. cor. of Second
and Tammany St., Phila?

BOSS
Chemical
WRITING
FLUID

Two labeled umbrella inks, aqua, 2-1/2", eight-sided, open pontil, rolled lip, American 1840-1860, **$400-$425**.

Umbrella Ink – J.W. Seaton / Louisville, KY, 2-1/8", light blue green, 10-sided, open pontil, rough inward rolled lip, American 1840-1860, **$800-$900.**

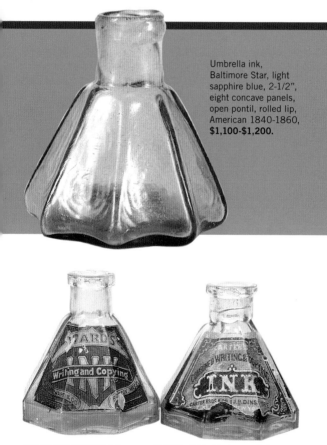

Umbrella ink, Baltimore Star, light sapphire blue, 2-1/2", eight concave panels, open pontil, rolled lip, American 1840-1860, **$1,100-$1,200.**

Two labeled umbrella inks, aqua, 2-3/8", eight-sided, smooth base, tooled top, American 1865-1880, **$200-$225.**

Lego's Cholera Syrup, aqua, 6-1/4", oval shape, open pontil, American 1840-1860, **$250-$300.**

Dr. D.C. Kellinger – Dr. Dewitt C. Kellinger's Liniment or Magic Fluid, blue aqua, 3-7/8", open pontil, American 1840-1860, **$175-$200.**

Hurd's Cough Balsam, blue aqua, 4-5/8", open pontil, American 1840-1860, **$150-$175.**

CHAPTER 11

Medicine Bottles

The medicine bottle group includes all pieces specifically made to hold patented medicines. Bitters and cures bottles, however, are excluded because the healing powers of these mixtures were questionable.

A patent medicine was one whose formula was registered with the U.S. Patent office, which opened in 1790. Not all medicines were patented, since the procedure required the manufacturer to reveal the medicine's contents. After the passage of the Pure Food and Drug Act of 1907, most of these patent medicine companies went out of business after they were required to list the ingredients of the contents on the bottle, and consumers learned that most medicines consisted of liquor diluted with water and an occasional pinch of opiates, strychnine, and arsenic. I have spent many enjoyable hours reading the labels on these bottles and wondering how anyone would survive after taking the recommended doses.

One of the oldest and most collectible medicine bottles was manufactured in England from 1723 and 1900—the embossed Turlington "Balsam of Life" bottle. The first embossed U.S. medicine bottle dates from around 1810. When searching out these bottles, always be on the lookout for embossing and original boxes. Embossed "Shaker" or "Indian" medicine bottles are collectible and valuable. Most embossed medicines made before 1840 are clear and aqua; the embossed greens, amber, and various shades of blues, specifically the darker cobalt blues, are much more collectible and valuable.

Dr. A.L. Adams Liver Balsam, deep blue, 7-1/2", full iron pontil, American 1840-1860, **$650-$700.**

Carter's Spanish Mixture, deep olive green, 8", iron pontil, American 1845-1865, **$550-$600.**

Dixie Tonic – Dr. Harters – Dr. Harter Medicine Co. – Dayton, Ohio, medium yellow amber, 7-1/2", smooth base, American 1885-1895, **$300-$400.**

Black Gin For The Kidneys – The Zoeller Medical Co. – Pittsburgh, PA, deep red amber, 9", smooth base, American 1880-1895, **$175-$200.**

Dr. Dewee's Worm Syrup –
P.T. Wright & Co. Phila, pale
aqua, 4", open pontil, rolled
lip, American 1840-1860,
$125-$150.

Dr. Clark, N. York, deep
emerald green, 9-1/4", iron
pontil, American 1845-1860,
$1,000-$1,100.

Dr. A.L. Adams – Liver Balsam, 7-1/2", deep blue
aqua, open pontil, applied tapered collar top,
American 1840-1860, **$600-$700.**

Dr. Owens London Horse Linament – Clarkston – Michigan, deep blue aqua, 5-3/8", open pontil, American 1840-1860, **$350-$375.**

Dr. Townsend's Expectorant Syrup, pale aqua, 5-3/4", open pontil, American 1840-1860, **$400-$450.**

Dr. Birmingham's Anti Billious – Blood Purifier, 8-5/8", medium emerald green, 9 indented panels, smooth base, applied top, American 1865-1880, **$800-$900.**

Hufeland's Life Cordial, medium yellow green, 7-1/8", open pontil, American 1840-1860, **$750-$800.**

M.B. Robert's Vegetable Embrocation, medium teal blue, 5-1/4", open pontil, American 1840-1860, **$300-$325.**

Reed's Gilt 1878 Hair Tonic, medium amber, 8-3/4", label, American 1875-1885, **$250-$275.**

Smith's Anodyne Cough Drops – Montpelier, aqua, 5-7/8", open pontil, American 1840-1860, **$600-$650.**

Thomson's Compound Syrup Of Tar For Consumption – Philada, deep blue aqua, 5-3/4", open pontil, American 1840-1860, **$125-$150.**

Dr. Friend's Cough Balsam – Morristown, N.J., blue aqua, 6-1/8", open pontil, American 1840-1860, **$450-$500.**

True Daffy's Elixir – Unless The Name – Of Dicey & Co. – Is In the Stamp – Over The Cork   The Medicine Is Counterfeit – Dicey & Co./ No. 10 Bow / Church Yard London, 5", pale green, pontil scarred base, applied double collar top, English 1840-1860, **$700-$800.**

T. Morris Perot & Co – Druggists – Philada, 5-1/4", light cobalt blue, open pontil, inward rolled lip, American 1840-1860, **$700-800.**

E. A. Buckhout's / Dutch / Liniment (Portly Standing Dutchman) Prepared At Mechanicville / Saratoga Co. N.Y., 4-3/4", open pontil, inward rolled lip, American 1840-1860, **$350-$400.**

Christies Aque Balsam – New York, 7", aqua blue, iron pontil, applied double collar top, American 1840-1860, **$350-$400.**

I. Sutton & Co., Covington, KY, medium cobalt blue, 8-1/2", American 1840-1860, **$800-$1,200.**

Massena Spring Water, golden yellow amber, quart, American 1880-1885, **$250-$375.**

CHAPTER 12

Mineral Water Bottles

The drinking of water from mineral springs was very popular for a full century with the peak period falling between 1860 and 1900. Consequently, most collectible bottles were produced during these years. While the earliest bottles are pontilled, the majority of them are smooth based. The sources of these natural waters came from various springs that were high in carbonates (alkaline), sulfurous compounds, various salts, and often carbonated naturally. The waters were also thought to possess medical and therapeutic qualities and benefits. Spring water was also another popular name often used for natural or unaltered mineral water.

Kissingen Water – T.H.D. – The Spa Phila, medium olive yellow, half-pint, smooth base, American 1870-1880, **$250-$275.**

Although the shapes and sizes of mineral bottles are not very creative, the lettering and design, both embossed and paper, are bold and interesting. Mineral bottles can range in size from seven inches up to 14 inches. Most were cork-stopped, manufactured in a variety of colors, and embossed with the name of the glasshouse manufacturer. In order to withstand the strong gaseous pressures of the contents and the severe high pressure bottling process, most bottles produced were manufactured with heavy, thick glass and were reused as often as possible.

Adirondack Spring –
Whitehall – N.Y., deep blue
green, pint, smooth base,
American 1865-1875,
$175-$200.

Avon – Spring Water, blue
aqua, quart, smooth base,
American 1865-1875,
$450-$475.

A. Schroth – Sch,ll Haven (in
slug plate) – Superior Mineral
Water – Union Glass Works,
deep cobalt blue, 7-1/2", iron
pontil, American 1840-1860,
$1,600-$1,800.

Bakers Mineral Waters –
Louisville – B, medium blue
green, 7-3/8", iron pontil,
American 1840-1860,
$200-$225.

Blue Lick (motif of stag)
Water – Hamilton, Gray & Co.
– Proprietors – Maysville KY,
dark amber, 9-3/8", smooth
base, American 1865-1875,
$1,700-$1,800.

Caladonia – Spring – Wheelock
VT., golden amber in lower
half shading to a yellow in
the shoulders, quart, smooth
base, American 1865-1875,
$450-$500.

Clarke & Co. – New York,
medium blue green, quart, iron
pontil, American 1850-1860,
$350-$437.

Deep Rock Spring – Oswego,
N.Y., medium teal blue green,
quart, smooth base, American
1865-1875, **$1,900-$2,000.**

Excelsior – Spring – Saratoga N.Y., emerald green, quart, smooth base, American 1865-1875, **$150-$175.**

Geo. Upp Jr. – York, PA – Mineral Water, deep cobalt blue, 7-5/8", iron pontil, American 1840-1860, **$900-$1,000.**

Geo. W. Felix – M.W. – Harrisburg – PA – Superior – F – Mineral Waters, cobalt blue, 7-3/8", iron pontil, American 1840-1860, **$1,500-$1,600.**

Geyser Spring – Saratoga Springs – New York-Avery N. Lord – 66 Broad St. – Utica. N.Y., aqua, quart, smooth base, American 1865-1875, **$800-$900.**

Hanbury Smith – N.Y. –
Congress Water, yellow olive
green, pint, smooth base,
American 1865-1875,
$1,800-$1,900.

J & L Bender – Lock Haven – PA
(in slug plate) – Mineral Water,
deep blue green, 7-1/2", iron
pontil, American 1840-1860,
$1,000-$1,100.

Glacier Spouting Spring – Saratoga / Springs, N.Y., pint, blue aqua,
smooth base, applied double collar top, American 1865-1875,
$2,700-$2,900.

Deep Rock Spring – Oswego, N.Y., pint, medium teal blue, smooth base, applied double collar top, American 1865-1875, **$150-$175.**

J. Mason – Utica – Mineral Waters – J.M. & Co., 7-1/4", medium green, iron pontil, applied tapered collar top, American 1840-1860, **$600-$700.**

Gettysburg Katalysine Water, quart, yellow olive green, smooth base, applied double collar top, American 1865-1875, **$600-$700.**

Iodine Spring Water / L / South Hero, VT, quart, yellow amber, smooth base, applied double collar top, American 1865-1875, **$1,100-$1,200.**

Poison – The Owl Drug
Co. – Aqua Ammonia
Poison, deep cobalt
blue, 9-5/8", American
1890-1910, **$100-$125.**

CHAPTER 13

Poison Bottles

By the very nature of their contents, poison bottles form a unique category for collecting. While most people assume that poison bottles are plain, most are very decorative, making them easy to identify their toxic contents. In 1853, the American Pharmaceutical Association recommended that laws be passed requiring identification of all poison bottles. In 1872, the American Medical Association recommended that poison bottles be identified with a rough surface on one side and the word poison on the other. But as so often happened during that era, the passing of these laws was very difficult and the manufacturers were left to do whatever they wanted. Because a standard wasn't established, a varied group of bottle shapes, sizes, and patterns were manufactured including skull and crossbones, or skulls, leg bones, and coffins.

These bottles were manufactured with quilted or ribbed surfaces and diamond/lattice-type patterns for identification by touch. Colorless bottles are very rare since most poison bottles were produced in dark shades of blues and browns, another identification aid. When collecting these bottles, caution must be exercised since it is not uncommon to find a poison bottle with its original contents. If the bottle has the original glass stopper, the value and demand for the bottle will greatly increase.

Bowman's Drug Stores – Poison, cobalt blue, 7-1/2", original label, American 1890-1920, **$550-$600.**

The J.F. Hartz Co. – Limited – Toronto, deep cobalt blue, 7-7/8", Canadian 1890-1910, rare in large size, **$600-$650.**

Three poison "The Owl Drug Co." bottles, cobalt blue, 4", 5-3/4", and 6-5/8", American 1915-1920, **$250-$275.**

Poison-Poison, red amber,
10-1/4", American 1890-1910,
$90-$100.

"Poison (motif of star above
and a skull and crossed bones
below) Poison," yellow amber,
4-5/8", American 1890-1910,
$300-$350.

Pair of Owl Drug bottles, medium amber, 3-1/4" and 4-1/2",
American 1890-1920, **$125-$150.**

Labeled three-sided poison bottle, cobalt blue, 5-1/4", tooled top, American 1890-1910, **$125-$150.**

"Poison (motif of skull and crossbones) – DP – Poison," cobalt blue, 2-7/8", American 1890-1910, **$600-$650.**

Diamond and Quilt Pattern Poison, 13", Gallon, Deep Cobalt Blue, smooth base (U.S.P.H.S), tooled wide top, American 1890-1910, **$2,400-$2,500.**

Pair of poison bottles, emerald green, 5-1/2", American 1890-1920, **$140-$160.**

Three poison bottles, cobalt blue, 2-3/4", 3-1/2", and 5", American 1890-1920, **$100-$125.**

Coffin Poison – Poison –Poison, 7-1/2", Cobalt Blue, smooth base (Norwich 16A), tooled top, American 1890-1910, **$600-$650**.

Poison – Poison, 7-7/8", Yellow Green, Square Form, smooth base (CIO), tooled top, American 1890-1910, **$2,500-$3,000**.

Diamond and Quilt Pattern Poison, 2-1/2", original label reads: 'Dispensary Tablets/ Atropine / Sulfate / 1-2 Grain / Poison', smooth base, tooled top, American 1890-1910, **$50-$75.**

Bowman's Drug Stores – Poison, cobalt blue, 4", original label, American 1890-1920, **$300-$325.**

Poison –The Owl Drug Co.,-Single Winged Owl Perched on a Mortar and Pestle, 9-1/2", Cobalt Blue, Triangular Form, smooth base, tooled top, American 1890-1915, **$1,000-$1,200.**

California Natural Seltzer Water / H&G, 7-1/2", rare color, American 1875-1880, **$3,000-$4,000.**

CHAPTER 14

Soda Bottles

After years of selling, buying, and trading, I have come to believe that soda bottles support one of the largest collector groups in the United States. Even collectors who don't normally seek out soda bottles always seem to have a few on their tables for sale (or under the table).

Soda is basically artificially flavored or unflavored carbonated water. In 1772, an Englishman named Joseph Priestley succeeded in defining the process of carbonation. Small quantities of unflavored soda were sold by Professor Benjamin Silliman in 1806. By 1810, New York druggists were selling homemade seltzer as a cure-all for stomach problems with flavors being added to the solution in the mid 1830s. By 1881, flavoring was a standard additive in these seltzers.

Because of pressure caused by carbonation, bottle manufacturers had to use a much stronger type of bottle, which eventually led to the heavy-walled blob-type soda bottle. Some of these more common closures were the Hutchinson-Type Wire Stoppers, Lightning Stoppers, and Cod Stoppers.

Soda bottles generally aren't unique in design, since the manufacturers had to produce them as cheaply as possible to keep up with demand. The only way to distinguish among bottles is by the lettering, logos, embossing, or labels (not very common).

W. Ryer – R (in script) – Union Glass Works – Philada, deep cobalt blue, 7-3/8", American 1840-1860, **$250-$300.**

Brutche & Tuchshmit – Newport, KY, deep blue aqua, 7-1/2", American 1840-1860, **$90-$100.**

C. Smith, cobalt blue, 7-3/8", American 1840-1860, **$300-$325.**

C. M. Walter – M. Holly – N.J. (in a slug plate), light blue green, 7", American 1840-1860, **$350-$375.**

Dean & Paxton – Newark – N.J., light blue green, 6-5/8", American 1840-1860, **$200-$225.**

E.I. Stahl – Newark – N.J., medium blue green, 7-1/8", American 1840-1860, **$800-$900.**

F & L Schaum – Baltimore – Glass Works, deep olive green, 7-1/4", American 1840-1860, **$450-$475.**

G.A. Kohl – Easton, PA – Improved – K – Patent, medium emerald green, 7-1/2", American 1840-1860, **$100-$125.**

Geo. Keilmann – Tamaqua – PA (in a slug plate), medium blue green, 7-3/8", American 1855-1870, **$450-$475.**

Geo. W. Hoffman – Allentown – PA, medium blue green, 7-1/8", American 1855-1865, **$90-$100.**

Harrisburg Bottling Works – Harrisburg, PA (in a slug plate), yellow olive, 8-5/8", American 1855-1865, **$450-$500.**

Glow & Co. / New Castle, 7-1/2", Deep Blue Aqua, iron pontil, applied tapered collar top, American 1840-1860, **$250-$300.**

J. Rother, black amethyst, 9", 10-pin shape, American 1855-1865, **$6,500-$7,000.**

John J. Staff, dark olive amber (black), 7-1/8", American 1860-1870, **$450-$475.**

John McKeon – Washington – D.C., medium blue green, 7-1/4", American 1840-1860, **$1,200-$1,300.**

Keller & Velten – Louisville, KY., light green, 7-1/8", 10-sided, American 1860-1870, **$400-$500.**

Louis Weber – Louisville – KY, medium amber, 7-1/8", American 1860-1870, **$100-$125.**

M. Prickitt / Pleasant Mills / NJ, 7-1/8", medium blue green, iron pontil, applied double collar top, American 1840-1860, **$1,500-$1,600.**

R.W. Babington – Chester – N.J., medium emerald green, 7-1/4", American 1840-1860, **$900-$1,000.**

I. Sutton – Cincinnati, deep cobalt blue, 7-3/8", American 1840-1860, **$250-$300.**

W.P Knicker – Bocker – Soda Water- 164, 18th St. N.Y. 1848, 7-3/8", 10-sided, deep cobalt blue, iron pontil, applied blob top, American 1848-1860, **$300-$400.**

McKay & Clark – No. 130 – Franklin St. – Balt., medium blue green, 8-1/2", 10-pin shape, American 1855-1865, **$1,300-$1,400.**

M. Richardson – Lockport, blue aqua, 7-1/4", American 1840-1860, **$450-$500.**

Target ball, Sophienhutte In Ilmenau (Thur), 2-5/8"
diameter, German 1880-1900, **$550-$600.**

CHAPTER 15

Target Balls

Target balls are small rounded balls the approximate size of a major league baseball and were initially hand blown into a three-piece mold. Another type of target ball is the range ball that was often as small as a golf ball and placed on top of a metal pole as a stationary target.

Most of the common balls have a sheared or sharp-edged neck caused by tearing the ball from the blowpipe before the ball had properly cooled. Then the balls were filled with confetti, ribbon, or other materials such as sawdust or wood shavings. Also, the color differences happened when the batch of glass used in the previous day's production was not entirely used and cleaned properly, and the next day's glass color would be tinted from the previous batch of glass. In addition, clear glass wasn't popular, since it was hard to see when projected into the air. Some of the most popular colors were amber, various shades of light blue, purple (amethyst), and green.

Used for target practice from the 1850s to early 1900s, they gained considerable popularity during the 1860s and 1870s in exhibitions and Wild West shows with Buffalo Bill Cody and Annie Oakley until the 1920s. During one summer, the Bohemian Glass Works manufactured target balls at the rate of 1,250,000 over a six-month period. Others such as Adam H. Bogardus and Ira Paine's had their target balls manufactured by various glassmakers throughout the country, as well as Europe and especially England.

Around 1900, clay pigeons started to be used in lieu of target balls. Because target balls were made to be broken, they are extremely difficult to find, and have become rare, collectible, and valuable.

Bogardus Glass Ball Patd. April 10 1877 – 2-5/8" diameter, overall diamond pattern above and below embossed center band, rough sheared lip, American 1877-1900, **$300-$350.**

Target ball, bright yellow, 2-1/2" diameter, Czechoslovakian 1890-1910, **$100-$125.**

Target ball, Dr. A. Frank Glasshutten – Charlottenburg, yellow olive, 2-5/8" diameter, German 1890-1910, **$200-$225.**

Target ball, dark amethyst (black), 2-5/8" diameter, German 1890-1910, **$300-$350.**

Target ball, deep cobalt blue, 2-5/8" diameter, Australian 1880-1900, **$2,000-$2,100.**

Target ball, N.B. Glassworks Perth – N.B. Glass Works Perth, light sapphire blue, 2-5/8" diameter, English 1880-1900, **$100-$125.**

Target ball, IRA Paines Filled Ball Oct 23, 1877, cobalt blue, 2-5/8"
diameter, American 1877-1895, **$2,000-$2,100.**

Target ball (motif of man shooting on two sides), medium amethyst,
2-5/8" diameter, English 1877-1895, **$200-$250.**

Great Western/ Glass Ball – Manufacturing/ Company- Pittsburgh, PA-
2-5/8" diameter, yellow amber, rough sheared lip, American 1880-
1900, **$4,500-$5,000.**

Target Ball – 2-5/8" dia., medium Cobalt Blue, embossed center band
and overall square pattern, rough sheared lip, English 1880-1900,
$200-$225.

Target Ball – 'Sept 9 1879/ CTB (Composite Target Ball Company)
/Patented / CO / MAR 9 1880 (on base), 3" diameter, black
composite ball, Rough Top, American 1880-1900, **$275-$300
(scarce).**

For Hockeys Patent Trap – 2-1/2" diameter, medium grass green, rough sheared lip, English 1880-1900, **$1,000–$1,200.**

IRA Paine's Filled – Ball Pat Apl'D For – 2-5/8" diamond, yellow amber, rough sheared lip, American 1877-1900, **$400-$450.**

Special style violin
bottle, amber,
$150-$250.

CHAPTER 16

Violin and Banjo Bottles

While roaming the aisles of bottle and antiques shows, I have often seen a violin- or banjo-shaped bottle on a table, admired its shape and color, then set it back down and moved on to whiskey and medicine bottles. I didn't fully appreciate these uniquely shaped bottles until I attended the June 1999 National Bottle Museum Antique Bottle Show in Saratoga, New York, to participate in a book signing.

Before the show, a silent auction was held that included a spectacular display of violin and banjo bottles. At that time, I had the pleasure of meeting several knowledgeable collectors and members of the Violin Bottle Collectors Association and received a short lesson and history of violin bottles. With the help of many dedicated members of the Violin Bottle Collectors Association, we've written a chapter that will assist both the veteran and the novice collector with understanding the fun and collecting of violin and banjo bottles.

While gathering the information for this chapter, it became clear that the majority of bottle and antiques collectors and dealers (including this collector) had little knowledge about violin and banjo bottles and their beginnings. Are they considered antiques? How old is a violin bottle? Why and where were they manufactured?

First, most were manufactured in the 20th century, with heavy production not taking place until the 1930s. One interesting aspect about violin and banjo bottles is that they are completely original designs and not copied from

Large banjo (LB1-9"), green, **$75-$125.**

any earlier bottle types, such as historic flasks and bitters. This makes these bottles antiques, in that they are the first of their design and style.

As with other specialty groups, violin and banjo bottles have specific categories and classes, and codes with each category. For the serious collector, I recommend *The Classification of Violin Shaped Bottles*, 2nd Edition, 1999, and 3rd Edition, 2004, by Robert A. Linden (dorall114@aol.com) and *Violin Bottles, Banjos, Guitars, and Other Novelty Glass*, 1995, by Don and Doris Christensen. Information on the association can be obtained by writing to the Violin Bottle Collector's Association, C/O Meg Stevens (membership director), 13 Whipple Tree Rd., Ballston Spa, NY 12020 or at pook@nycap.rr.com or Samia Koudsi (president) at s.koudsi@mchsi.com.

Selection of Bard's Town violin bottles, **$50-$75 each**.
Top: Bard's Town, 1939, 5"; Bard's Town, 1940, 4-7/8"
Bottom: Bard's Town, 1938, 4-7/8"; Bard's Town Bond, 1940, 4-7/8"; Bourbon Springs, 1938, 4-7/8".

Large violin bottle
(LV1a3), cobalt
blue, **$50-$100**.

Large violin bottle
(LV5), yellow,
$100-$120.

Selection of Bard's Town violin bottles, **$50-$75 each**.
Top: Bourbon Springs, 1939, 4-7/8"; Old Anthem Brand, 1938, 4-7/8"
Bottom: Old Bard Brand, 1938, 4-7/8"; Old Fiddle, 1950, 4-3/4"; Old
Fiddle, 1950, 4-3/4".

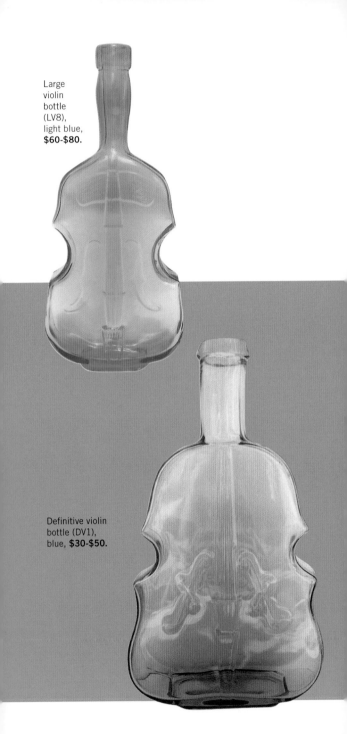

Large violin bottle (LV8), light blue, $60-$80.

Definitive violin bottle (DV1), blue, $30-$50.

French violin bottle (FV1-3), blue tint, **$40-$60**; green tint, **$40-$60**; light peach, **$50-$75.**

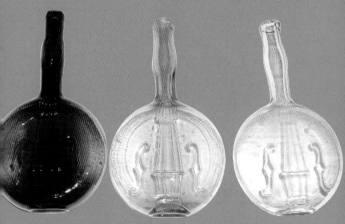

Small banjo (SB1-7"), amethyst, **$25-$50**; green, **$75-$100**; blue, **$25-$50.**

Definitive violin bottles (DV 2 and 3), ruby red, each **$60-$100.**

Violin bottle (EV) with tuning pegs, or "ears," cobalt blue, **$10-$20.**

Large banjo (LB4 and 5, 9-1/2"),
blue, amethyst, green, **$25-$40.**

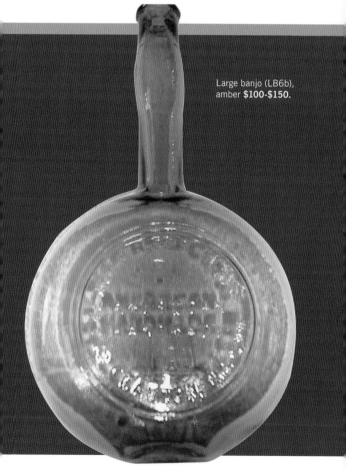

Large banjo (LB6b),
amber **$100-$150.**

Star Whiskey / New York / W.B. Crowell Jr., 8-1/2", American 1860-1875, **$500-$800.**

CHAPTER 17

Whiskey Bottles

Whiskeys, sometimes referred to as spirits, come in an array of sizes, designs, shapes, and colors. The whiskey bottle dates back to the 19th century and provides the avid collector with numerous examples of rare and valuable pieces.

In 1860, E. G. Booz manufactured a whiskey bottle in the design of a cabin embossed with year 1840 and the words "Old Cabin Whiskey." One theory has it that the word booze was derived from his name to describe hard liquor. The Booz bottle is also given the credit of being the first to emboss the name on whiskey bottles.

After the repeal of Prohibition in 1933, the only inscription that could be found on any liquor bottles was "Federal Law Forbids Sale or Re-use of This Bottle," which was continued through 1964.

Three tooled top amber whiskeys: Coblantz & Levy – 164 &166 2nd St. – Portland – Oregon, 11-1/8", 1900-1910; Cerruti Merchantile Co. Inc. – S.F. Cal., 11-3/8", 1905-1915; Rathjen Mercantile Co. – R.M.C. – S.F. Cal., 1907-1908, **$175-$200.**

Remington Liquor Co. Distilled Just Right – 101 Third St. – Portland Ore., medium amber, 12", American 1900-1910, **$175-$200.**

Golden Rule – XXXX – Whiskey – Braunschweiger & Co. Inc. – S.F. Cal., medium amber, 11-5/8", American 1895-1905, **$200-$225.**

James Kerr – 1628 Market St. – Gibbons Old Rye – A Specialty – Philada. PA, amber, quart, 9-1/4", American 1875-1890, **$200-$225.**

Old Wheat – 1835 – Whiskey (inside embossed oval), medium copper amber, 11-3/4", American 1865-1875, **$250-$300.**

Parole – Pure (motif of standing horse) – Rye – Whiskey, yellow amber, quart, 10-1/8", American 1875-1880, **$350-$400.**

Pepper – Hand Made – Sour Mash – Whiskey (in a circle) – Carroll & Carroll – Sole Agents – S.F. Cal., light amber, 11-3/4", American 1890-1902, **$350-$375.**

Handled whiskey, Wharton's – Whiskey – 1850 – Chestnut Grove – Whitney Glass Works – Glassboro NJ, medium amber, 10-1/8", American 1860-1870, **$900-$1,000.**

Whiskey cylinder, deep blue green, 10-1/2", American 1865-1875, **$180-$190.**

Whiskey cylinder, Dyottville Glass Works Phila (on base), medium cherry puce, 11-1/2", American 1855-1870, **$150-$175.**

Teakettle – Trade Mark (inside the motif of a teakettle) – Old Bourbon – Shea, Bocqueraz & McKee – Agents – San Francisco, golden amber, 12", American 1873-1885, **$800-$850.**

Turkish Wine – Goodwin & Edgerly – New York, medium yellow green, 9-7/8", American 1865-1875, **$750-$800.**

Wolters Bros & Co – 115 and 117 – Front St. – S.F., 12", medium amber, smooth base, applied top, American 1886-1895, **$375-$400.**

E.G. Booz's – Old Cabin – Whiskey-1840 – E.G. Booz's/Old Cabin/Whiskey-120 Walnut St./Philadelphia, 7-7/8", amber, smooth base, applied tapered collar top, American 1860-1870, **$1,800-$2,000.**

E. Commins & Co. – EC & CO (monogram) – San Francisco, Cal, 11-1/2 ½", red amber, smooth base, applied top, American 1885-1891, **$350-$400.**

Old Wheat – S.M & Co – Whiskey, 11", yellow amber, pontil scarred base, applied double collar top, American 1050 1866, **$300-$350.**

Pacific Glass Works S.F. (Embossed on base), 11-1/4", smooth base, applied double collar top, blown in a 3-piece mold, American 1860-1875, very rare, **$3,000-$3,300**.

S.S. Smith. Jr. & Co. – Cincinnati, O., 9-3/4", medium cobalt blue, semi-cabin shape, smooth base, applied top, American 1865-1875, **$1,800-$2,000**.

Digging for Bottles

There are many ways to begin your search to be a picker or collector, but digging up bottles yourself can be exciting. The adventure of the hunt is as cool as the actual find. The efforts of individual and bottle club digging expeditions have turned up numerous important historical finds. These digs surfaced valuable information about the early decades of our country and the history of bottle and glass manufacturing in the United States. The following points cover the essentials: locating the digging sites, equipment and tools, general rules and helpful hints, as well as a section on privy/outhouse digging.

LOCATING THE DIGGING SITE

Prior to any dig, you will need to learn as much as possible about the area you plan to explore. Do not overlook valuable resources in your own community. You will can collect important information from your local library, local and state historical societies, various types of maps, and city directories (useful for information about people who once lived on a particular piece of property) and of course the internet. The National Office of Cartography in Washington D.C. and the National Archives are also excellent resources.

In my experience, old maps are the best guides for locating digging areas with good potential. These maps show what the town looked like in early era and provides clues to where trading posts/general stores, saloons, hotels, red light districts, and the town dump were located. The two types of maps which will prove most useful are the Plat maps and Sanborn Fire Insurance maps.

A Plat map, which will show every home and business in the city or area you wish to dig, can be compared to current maps to identify the older structures or determine where they once stood. The Sanborn Insurance maps are the most detailed, accurate, and helpful of all for choosing a digging site providing detailed information on illustrating the location of houses, factories, cisterns, wells, privies, streets, and property lines. These maps were produced for nearly every city and town between

1867 to 1920 and are dated so that it's possible to determine the age of the sites you're considering. Another new tool in the hunt for surveying remote digging sites is Google Earth. It allows you to view the entire site from space.

The illustration shown below depicts an 1890 Sanborn Perris map section of East Los Angeles that was used to locate an outhouse in East Los Angeles, circa 1885-1905, that uncovered more than fifty bottles. Knowing the appropriate age of the digging site also helps to determine the age and types of bottles or artifacts you find there.

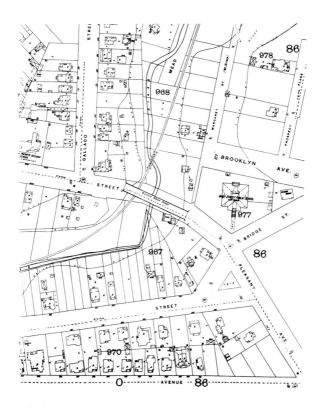

Sanborn Perris map section of East Lost Angeles, 1885-1905.

Local Chambers of Commerce, law enforcement agencies, and residents who have lived in the community for a number of years can be very helpful in your in search for information. Other great resource for publications about the area's history are local antique and gift shops, which often carry old books, maps, and other literature on the town, county, and surrounding communities.

Since most early settlers handled garbage themselves, buried bottles can be unearthed almost anywhere, but a little thinking can narrow the search to a location to holding treasures. Usually, the garbage was hauled and dumped within one mile of the town limits. Often, settlers or store owners would dig a hole about twenty-five yards out from the back of their home or business for garbage and refuse. Many hotels and saloons had a basement or underground storage area where empty bottles were kept.

Ravines, ditches, and washes are also prime digging spots because heavy rains or melting snow often washed debris down from other areas. Bottles can quite often be found beside houses and under porches where residents would store or throw their bottles in the late 19th and 20th centuries. Explore abandoned roads where houses or cabins once stood, wagon trails, old railroad tracks, and sewers. If it is legal, old battlegrounds and military encampments are excellent places to dig. Cisterns and wells are other good sources of bottles and period artifacts.

The first love of this bottle hound is an expedition to a Ghost town. It's not only fun but a valuable lesson in history. The best places to search in Ghost towns are near saloons, trade stores, and the red light district, train stations, and the town dump (prior to 1900). The Tonopah, Nevada town dump was the start of my digging experiences and is still a favorite spot.

PRIVY/OUTHOUSE DIGGING

"You've dug bottles out of an old outhouse? You've got to be kidding!" Telling your family and friends about this unique experience will usually kick the conversation into high gear. Privy's are one of the best places to find old bottles that can be very rare and in great condition. Prior to 1870, most bottles were not hauled out to the dump. Why would anybody bother when they could simply toss old bottles down the outhouse hole in the back of a house or business? In fact, very few pontil age (pre-Civil War) bottles are ever found in dumps. At that time people either dug a pit in their backyard for trash, or, used the outhouse. These outhouses, or privies, have been know to yield all kinds of other artifacts such as guns, coins, knives, crockery, dishes, marbles, pipes, and other household items.

To develop a better sense of where privies can be found, it is important to have an understanding of their construction and uses. The privies of the nineteenth century which produce the best results were deep holes constructed with wood, brick, or sides called "liners". You'll find privies in a variety of shapes; square, round, rectangular, and oval.

In general, privies in cities are fairly deep and usually provide more bottles and artifacts. Privies in rural areas are shallower and do not contain as many bottles. Farm privies outhouses are very difficult to locate and digs often produce few results. How long was an outhouse used? Well, the life span of a privy is anywhere from ten to twenty years. It was possible to extend its useful life by cleaning it out or relining it with new wood, brick, or stone. In fact, nearly all older privies show some evidence of cleaning.

At some point, old privies were filled and abandoned. The fill materials included ashes, bricks, plaster, sand, rocks, building materials, or soil which had been dug out when a new or additional privy was added to the house. Often, bottles or other artifacts were thrown in with the fill. The depth of the privy determined the amount of the fill required. In any case, the result was a privy filled with layers of various materials with the bottom layer being the "use" layer or "trash" layer.

It is possible to locate these old outhouses due to the characteristic differences in density and composition of the undisturbed earth. Because of the manner of construction, it is easy to locate them by probing the area with a metal rod or "probe" Your own community is a great place to begin the hunt for the privy. A good starting point is to find an old house dating back to 1880-1920 that usually had a least one privy. Try to locate a small lot with few buildings or obstructions to get in the way of your dig. The first thing to look for are depressions in the ground since materials used to fill privies have a tendency to settle, a subtle depression may indicate where a septic tank, well, or privy was once located. In addition, like most household dumps, outhouses were usually located between 15 to 30 yards behind a residence or business. Another good indicator of an old privy site is an unexpected grouping of vegetation such as bushes or trees which flourishes above the rich fertilized ground. Privies were sometimes located near old trees for shade and privacy.

The most common privy locations were (1) directly outside the back door, (2) along a property line, (3) in one of the back corners or the rear middle of the lot, and (4) the middle of the yard. Now that you've located that privy (with luck it's full of great bottles), its time to get down and dirty and open up the hole. The approximate dimensions of the hole can usually be determined with your probe. If you know, or even think, that the hole is deeper than you are tall, it is extremely important to avoid a cave-in by opening up the entire hole. Never attempt to try and dig half of the hole with hopes of getting to the trash layer quicker. Remember that the fill is looser than the surrounding ground and could come down on you. Also, always dig to the bottom and check the corners carefully. Privies were occasionally cleaned out but very often bottles and artifacts were missed that were in the corners or on the sides. If you are not sure whether you've hit the bottom, check with the probe. It's easier to determine if you can feel the fill below what you may think is the bottom. In brick and stone-lined holes, if the wall keeps going down, you are not on the bottom.

Quite often it is difficult to date a privy without the use of detailed and accurate maps. But it is possible to determine the age of the privy by the type and age of items found in the hole. The chart below lists some types of bottles you might find in a dig and shows how their age relates to the age of the privy.

Digging and refilling the hole can be hard work and very tiring. To help make this chore easier, put down a tarp on the ground surrounding the hole as you dig, and shovel the dirt on the tarp. Then, shovel the dirt off the tarp and fill five-gallon plastic buckets. The first benefit of this method is the time and energy you'll save filling the hole. The second benefit, and maybe the biggest, is that you'll leave no mess. This becomes important for building a relationship with the property owner. The less mess the more likely you'll get permission to dig again. Also, your dig will be safer and easier if you use a walk board. Take an 8-foot-long 2 x 8 plank and place it over the hole. The digger, who is standing on the board, pulling up buckets of dirt (let's all take turns), can do so without hitting the sides. This also reduces the risk of the bucket man falling in or caving in a portion of the hole. Setting up a tripod with a pulley over the hole will help to save time and prevent strain on the back. The short few paragraphs presented here are really just an outline of privy/outhouse digging.

THE PROBE

Regardless of whether you are digging in outhouses, old town dumps, or beneath a structure, a probe is an essential tool. It is usually five to six feet in length (depending on your height, a taller person may find that a longer probe will work better), with a handle made out of hollow or solid pipe, tapered to a point at the end so it's easier to penetrate the ground. Also, welding a ball bearing on the end of the rod will help in collecting soil samples. As discussed earlier, examining the soil samples is critical to finding privies. To make your probing easier, add some weight to the handle by filing the pipe with lead or welding a solid steel bar directly under the handle. The additional weight will reduce the effort needed to sink the probe.

While probing, press down slowly and try to feel for differences in the consistency of the soil. Unless you are probing into sand, you should reach a point at which it becomes difficult to push, a natural bottom. If you find you can probe deeper in an adjacent spot, you may have found an outhouse. When this happens, pull out the probe and plunge it in again, this time at an angle to see if you feel a brick or wood liner. After some practice, you'll be able to determine what type of material you are hitting. Glass, brick, crockery, and rocks all have their own distinctive sound and feel. While there are a number of places where you can purchase probes, you might want to have one custom made to conform to your body height and weight for more comfortable use.

DIGGING EQUIPMENT AND TOOLS

When I first started digging, I took only a shovel and my luck. I learned I was doing things the hard way, and, the result was a few broken bottles. Since then, I've refined my list of tools and equipment. The following list includes those items that I've found useful and recommended by veteran diggers.

GENERAL DIGGING EQUIPMENT

- Probe
- Long handled shovel
- Short handled shovel
- Potato rake-long handled
- Small hand rake
- Old table knives
- Old spoons
- Hard and soft bristle brushes
- Gloves/boots/eye protection/durable clothes
- Insect repellent, snake bite kit, first aid kit
- Extra water and hat
- Dirt sifter (for coins or other items, a 2ft x 2ft wooden frame with chicken wire).
- Hunting knife
- Boxes for packing and storing bottles

GENERAL RULES AND HELPFUL HINTS

Although I said there were no rules to bottle collecting, where digging there are two major rules you always need to follow.

RULE NO. 1:

Always be responsible and respectful and ask for permission to dig. As a safety precaution, do not leave any holes open over night. Do not damage shrubs, trees, or flowers unless the owner approves. When the digging is complete, always leave the site looking better that when you started. That means filling in all holes and raking over the area. Take out your trash as well as trash left by previous prospectors or others. Always offer to give the owner some of the bottles. They may not want any, but they will appreciate the gesture. If you adhere to these few rules, the community or owner will thank you and future bottle diggers will be welcomed.

RULE NO. 2:

Do not, under any circumstances, go digging alone. Ignoring this rule is extremely dangerous. When digging an outhouse, my recommendation is to go with no less than three people, and be sure to tell someone exactly where you're going and how long you expect to be gone. Remember, DON'T DIG ALONE.

When you start to dig, don't be discouraged if you don't find any bottles. If you unearth other objects such as coins, broken dishes, or bottle tops, continue to dig deeper and in a wider circle. When you do find that bottle, stop your digging and remove the surrounding dirt a little at a time with a small tool, brush, or spoon. Handle the bottle very carefully since old bottles are very fragile.

Now, that you know how to do it, what are you waiting for? Grab those tools, get those maps, and get started making the discoveries of a lifetime.

U.S. Trademarks

Trademarks are helpful for determining the history, age, and value of bottles. In addition, researching trademarks will give the bottle collector a deeper knowledge of the many glass manufacturers that produced bottles and the companies that provided the contents.

What is a trademark? By definition, a trademark is a word, name, letter, number, symbol, design, phrase, or a combination of all of these items that identifies and distinguishes a product from its competitors. For bottles, that mark usually appears on the bottom of the bottle and possibly on the label if a label still exists. Trademark laws only protect the symbol that represents the product, not the product itself.

Trademarks have been around for a long time. The first use of an identification mark on glassware was during the 1st century by glassmaker Ennion of Sidon and two of his students, Jason and Aristeas. They were the first glassmakers to identify their products by placing letters in the sides of their molds. In the 1840s, English glass manufacturers continued this practice using a similar technique.

Identifying marks have been found on antique Chinese porcelain, on pottery from ancient Greece and Rome, and on items from India dating back to 1300 B.C. In addition, stonecutter's marks have been found on many Egyptian structures dating back to 4000 B.C. In medieval times, craft and merchant owners relied on trademarks to distinguish their products from makers of inferior goods in order to gain buyers' loyalty. Trademarks were applied to almost everything, including paper, bread, leather goods, weapons, silver, and gold.

In the late 1600s, bottle manufacturers began to mark their products with a glass seal that was applied to the bottle while still hot. A die with the manufacturer's initials, date, or design was permanently molded on the bottles. This was both efficient and effective because cutting wasn't required, and the mark could be easily seen by the buyer.

Since the concept of trademarks spread beyond Europe, they were quickly adopted in North America as the number of immigrants grew. For many early trademark owners, protection for the trademark owner was almost nonexistent. While the U.S. constitution provided rights of ownership in copyrights and patents, there wasn't any trademark protection until Congress enacted the first federal trademark law in 1870. Significant revisions and changes were made to the 1870 trademark law in 1881, 1905, 1920, and 1946. Research indicates that registration of trademarks began in 1860 on glassware, with a major increase in the 1890s by all types of glass manufacturers.

DETERMINING BOTTLE MAKERS AND DATES

If you're able to determine the owner of a trademark, as well as when it might have been used, you will likely be able to determine the date of a piece. If the mark wasn't used long, it is much easier to pinpoint the bottle's age. If, however, the mark was used over an extended period of time, you will have to rely on additional references. Unfortunately, most numbers appearing with trademarks are not part of the trademark and, therefore, will not provide any useful information.

Approximately 1,200 trademarks have been created for bottles and fruit jars. Of these, 900 are older marks (1830s-1940) and 300 are more modern marks (1940s to 1970). Very few manufacturers used identical marks, which is amazing, considering how many companies have produced bottles.

Note: Words and letters in bold are the company's description with the trademarks as they appeared on the bottle. Each trademark is followed by the complete name and location of the company and the approximate period in which the trademark was used.

A: Adams & Co., Pittsburgh, PA, 1861-1891

A: John Agnew & Son, Pittsburgh, PA, 1854-1866

A: Arkansas Glass Container Corp., Jonesboro, AR, 1958-present (if machine made)

A (in a circle): American Glass Works, Richmond, VA, and Paden City, WV, 1908-1935

A & B together (AB): Adolphus Busch Glass Manufacturing Co, Belleville, IL, and St. Louis, MO, 1904-1907

ABC: Atlantic Bottle Co., New York City, NY, and Brackenridge, PA, 1918-1930

ABCo.: American Bottle Co., Chicago, IL, 1905-1916; Toledo, OH, 1916-1929

ABCO (in script): Ahrens Bottling Company, Oakland, CA, 1903-1908

A B G M Co.: Adolphus Busch Glass Manufacturing Co, Belleville, IL, 1886-1907; St. Louis, MO, 1886-1928

A & Co.: John Agnew and Co., Pittsburgh, PA, 1854-1892

A C M E: Acme Glass Co., Olean, NY, 1920-1930

A & D H C: A. & D.H. Chambers, Pittsburgh, PA, Union Flasks, 1843-1886

AGCo: Arsenal Glass Co. (or Works), Pittsburgh, PA, 1865-1868

AGEE and Agee (in script): Hazel Atlas Glass Co., Wheeling, WV, 1919-1925

AGNEW & CO.: Agnew & Co., Pittsburgh, PA, 1876-1886

AGWL, PITTS PA: American Glass Works, Pittsburgh, PA, 1865-1880; American Glass Works Limited, 1880-1905

AGW: American Glass Works, Richmond, VA, and Paden City, WV, 1908-1935

Ahrens Bottling (AB Co. in middle) Oakland Cal.: 1903-1908, listed in business directories as Diedrich Ahrens

Alabama Brewing (W over B in middle) San Francisco: 1899-1906

Albany Brewing (Trade AB Mark in middle): 1858-1918 (business ended with Prohibition)

AMF & Co.: Adelbert M. Foster & Co., Chicago, IL; Millgrove, Upland, and Marion, IN, 1895-1911

Anchor figure (with H in center): Anchor Hocking Glass Corp., Lancaster, OH, 1955

A. R. S.: A. R. Samuels Glass Co., Philadelphia, PA, 1855-1872

A S F W W Va.: A. S. Frank Glass Co., Wellsburg, WV, 1859

ATLAS: Atlas Glass Co., Washington, PA, and later Hazel Atlas Glass Co., 1896-1965

B: Buck Glass Co., Baltimore, MD, 1909-1961

B (in circle): Brockway Machine Bottle Co., Brockway, PA, 1907-1933

Ball and Ball (in script): Ball Bros. Glass Manufacturing Co., Muncie, IN, and later Ball Corp., 1887-1973

Baker Bros. Balto. MD.: Baker Brothers, Baltimore, MD, 1853-1905

BAKEWELL: Benjamin P. Bakewell Jr. Glass Co., 1876-1880

Baltimore Glass Works: 1860-1870

BANNER: Fisher-Bruce Co., Philadelphia, PA, 1910-1930

Beer Steam Bottling Company (WG & Son in diamond and W Goeppert & Son in middle) San Francisco: 1882-1886

BB Co: Berney-Bond Glass Co., Bradford, Clarion, Hazelhurst, and Smethport, PA, 1900

BB48: Berney-Bond Glass Co., Bradford, Clarion, Hazelhurst, and Smethport, PA, 1920-1930

BBCo: Bell Bottle Co, Fairmount, IN, 1910-1914

Bennett's: Gillinder & Bennett (Franklin Flint Glass Co.), Philadelphia, PA, 1863-1867

Bernardin (in script): W.J. Latchford Glass Co., Los Angeles, CA, 1932-1938

The Best: Gillender & Sons, Philadelphia, PA, 1867-1870

B F B Co.: Bell Fruit Bottle Co., Fairmount, IN, 1910

B. G. Co.: Belleville Glass Co., IL, 1882

Bishop's: Bishop & Co., San Diego and Los Angeles, CA, 1890-1920

BK: Benedict Kimber, Bridgeport and Brownsville, PA, 1825-1840

BLUE RIBBON: Standard Glass Co., Marion, IN, 1908

B. & M. S. Co: Bottler's & Manufacturer's Supply Company, Long Island City, NY 1904-1920. Mark seen on heel of New York City blob beer bottle.

Boca (BOB in a circle in middle) Beer: 1875-1891

BODE: Bode Extract Company, Chicago, IL. (Gustav Augustus Bode, proprietor). Mark seen on heel of Hutch Soda Bottles. Bode manufactured bottles from 1890 to 1892. He concentrated on production of extracts from 1892-1900; he passed away in 1900.

BOLDT: Charles Boldt Glass Manufacturing Co., Cincinnati, OH, and Huntington, WV, 1900-1929

Boyds (in script): Illinois Glass Co., Alton, IL, 1900-1930

BP & B: Bakewell, Page & Bakewell, Pittsburgh, PA, 1824-1836

Brelle (in script) Jar: Brelle Fruit Jar Manufacturing Co., San Jose, CA, 1912-1916

Brilliante: Jefferis Glass Co., Fairton, NJ, and Rochester, PA, 1900-1905

C (in a circle): Chattanooga Bottle & Glass Co. and later Chattanooga Glass Co., 1927-present

C (in a square): Crystal Glass Co., Los Angeles, CA, 1921-1929

C (in a star): Star City Glass Co., Star City, WV, 1949-present

C (in upside-down triangle): Canada Dry Ginger Ale Co., New York City, NY, 1930-1950

Canton Domestic Fruit Jar: Canton Glass Co., Canton, OH, 1890-1904

C & Co. or C Co: Cunninghams & Co., Pittsburgh, PA, 1880-1907

C. Beck, Santa Cruz: (Big Trees Brewery), 1894-1917

CCCo: Carl Conrad & Co., St. Louis, MO, (Beer), 1860-1883

C.V.Co. No. 1 & No 2: Milwaukee, WI, 1880-1881

C C Co.: Carl Conrad & Co., St. Louis, MO, 1876-1883

C C G Co.: Cream City Glass Co., Milwaukee, WI, 1888-1894

C.F.C.A.: California Fruit Canners Association, Sacramento, CA, 1899-1916

CFJCo: Consolidated Fruit Jar Co., New Brunswick, NJ, 1867-1882

C G I: California Glass Insulator Co., Long Beach, CA, 1912-1919

C G M Co: Campbell Glass Manufacturing Co., West Berkeley, CA, 1885

C G W: Campbell Glass Works, West Berkeley, CA, 1884-1885

C & H: Coffin & Hay, Hammonton, NJ, 1836-1838, or Winslow, NJ, 1838-1842

C & I: Cunningham & Ihmsen, Pittsburgh, PA, 1865-1879

C V No 2 — MILW: Chase Valley Glass Co. No 2, Milwaukee, WI, 1880-1881

C L G Co.: Carr-Lowrey Glass Co., Baltimore, MD, 1889-1920

CLARKE: Clarke Fruit Jar Co., Cleveland, OH, 1886-1889

CLIMAX: Fisher-Bruce Co, Philadelphia, PA, 1910-1930

CLOVER LEAF (in arch with picture of a clover leaf): 1890 (marked on ink and mucilage bottles)

Clyde, N. Y.: Clyde Glass Works, Clyde, NY, 1870-1882

The Clyde (in script): Clyde Glass Works, Clyde, NY, 1895

C. Milw: Chase Valley Glass Co., Milwaukee, WI, 1880-1881

Cohansey: Cohansey Glass Manufacturing Co., Philadelphia, PA, 1870-1900

CO-SHOE: Coshocton Glass Corp., Coshocton, OH, 1923-1928

C R: Curling, Robertson & Co., Pittsburgh, PA, 1834-1857, or Curling, Ringwalt & Co., Pittsburgh, PA, 1857-1863

CRYSTO: McPike Drug Co., Kansas City, MO, 1904

CS & Co: Cannington, Shaw & Co., St. Helens, England, 1872-1916

C.V.G.CO: Chase Valley Glass Company, Milwaukee, WI, 1880-1881

D (in a Keystone): Denver Glass Bottle Company, Denver, CO, 1946-1951

D 446: Consolidated Fruit Jar Co., New Brunswick, NJ, 1871-1882

DB: Du Bois Brewing Co., Pittsburgh, PA, 1918

Dexter: Franklin Flint Glass Works, Philadelphia, PA, 1861-1880

Diamond: (Plain) Diamond Glass Co., 1924-present

The Dictator: William McCully & Co., Pittsburgh, PA, 1855-1869

Dictator: William McCully & Co., Pittsburgh, PA, 1869-1885

Dillon G. Co.: Dillon Glass Company, Converse, IN, and Fairmount, IN, 1990-1894

D & O: Cumberland Glass Mfg. Co., Bridgeton, NJ, 1890-1900

D O C: D.O. Cunningham Glass Co., Pittsburgh, PA, 1883-1937

DOME: Standard Glass Co., Wellsburg, WV, 1891-1893

D S G Co.: De Steiger Glass Co., LaSalle, IL, 1879-1896

Duffield: Dr. Samuel Duffield, Detroit, MI, 1862-1866, and Duffield, Parke & Co., Detroit, MI, 1866-1875

Dyottsville: Dyottsville Glass Works, Philadelphia, PA, 1833-1923

E4: Essex Glass Co., Mt. Vernon, OH, 1906-1920

Economy (in script) TRADE MARK: Kerr Glass Manufacturing Co., Portland, OR, 1903-1912

Electric Trade Mark (in script): Gayner Glass Works, Salem, NJ, 1910

Electric Trade Mark: Gayner Glass Works, Salem, NJ, 1900-1910

Erd & Co., E R Durkee: E.R. Durkee & Co., New York, NY, Post-1874

The EMPIRE: Empire Glass Co., Cleveland, NY, 1852-1877

E R Durkee & Co: E.R. Durkee & Co., New York, NY, 1850-1860

E.S. & CO.: Evans, Sell & Company, Pittsburgh, PA, 1873-1877

Eureka 17: Eurkee Jar Co., Dunbar, WV, 1864

Eureka (in script): Eurkee Jar Co., Dunbar, WV, 1900-1910

Everett and EHE: Edward H. Everett Glass Co. (Star Glass Works), Newark, OH, 1893-1904

Everlasting (in script) JAR: Illinois Pacific Glass Co., San Francisco, CA, 1904

E W & Co: E. Wormser & Co., Pittsburgh, PA, 1857-1875

Excelsior: Excelsior Glass Co., St. John, Quebec, Canada, 1878-1883

F (inside a jar outline or keystone): C.L. Flaccus Glass Co., Pittsburgh, PA, 1900-1928

F WM. Frank & Sons: WM. Frank & Co., Pittsburgh, PA, 1846-1966, WM. Frank & Sons, Pittsburgh, PA, 1866-1876

F & A: Fahnstock & Albree, Pittsburgh, PA, 1860-1862

FERG Co: F.E. Reed Glass Co., Rochester, NY, 1898-1947

FF & Co: Fahnstock, Fortune & Co., Pittsburgh, PA, 1866-1873

F G: Florida Glass Manufacturing Co., Jacksonville, FL, 1926-1947

FL or FL & Co.: Frederick Lorenz & Co., Pittsburgh, PA, 1819-1841

FLINT–GREEN: Whitney Glass Works, Glassborough, NJ, 1888

FOLGER, JAF&Co., Pioneer, Golden Gate: J. A. Folger & Co., San Francisco, CA, 1850-present

G in circle (bold lines): Gulfport Glass Co., Gulfport, MS, 1955-1970

G E M: Hero Glass Works, Philadelphia, PA, 1884-1909

G & H: Gray & Hemingray, Cincinnati, OH, 1848-1851; Covington, KY, 1851-1864

G & S: Gillinder & Sons, Philadelphia, PA, 1867-1871 and 1912-1930

Geo. Braun Bottler (C over B in arrowhead in middle) 2219 Pine St. S.F.: 1893-1906

Gillinder: Gillinder Bros., Philadelphia, PA, 1871-1930

Gilberds: Gilberds Butter Tub Co., Jamestown, NY, 1883-1890

GLENSHAW (G in a box underneath name): Glenshaw Glass Co., Glenshaw, PA, 1904

GLOBE: Hemingray Glass Co., Covington, KY (the symbol "Parquet-Lac" was used beginning in 1895), 1886

Greenfield: Greenfield Fruit Jar & Bottle Co., Greenfield, IN, 1888-1912

G.W.: Great Western Glass Company, St. Louis, MO, 1874-1886

GWK & Co.: George W. Kearns & Co., Zanesville, OH, 1848-1911

H and H (in heart): Hart Glass Manufacturing Co., Dunkirk, IN, 1918-1938

H (with varying numerals): Holt Glass Works, West Berkeley, CA, 1893-1906

H (in a diamond): A.H. Heisey Glass Co., Oakwood Ave., Newark, OH, 1893-1958

H (in a triangle): J. T. & A. Hamilton Co., Pittsburgh, PA, 1900

Hamilton: Hamilton Glass Works, Hamilton, Ontario, Canada, 1865-1872

Hansen & Kahler (H & K in middle) Oakland Cal.: 1897-1908

Hazel: Hazel Glass Co., Wellsburg, WV, 1886-1902

H.B.Co: Hagerty Bros. & Co., Brooklyn, NY, 1880-1900

Helme: Geo. W. Helme Co., Jersey City, NJ, 1870-1895

Hemingray: Hemingray Brothers & Co. and later Hemingray Glass Co., Covington, KY, 1864-1933

Henry Braun (beer bottler in middle) Oakland Cal.: 1887-1896

H. J. Heinz: H.J. Heinz Co., Pittsburgh, PA, 1860-1869

Heinz & Noble: H.J. Heinz Co., Pittsburgh, PA, 1869-1872

F. J. Heinz: H.J. Heinz Co., Pittsburgh, PA, 1876-1888

H. J. Heinz Co.: H.J. Heinz Co., Pittsburgh, PA, 1888-present

HELME: Geo. W. Helme Co., NJ, 1870-1890

HERO: Hero Glass Works, Philadelphia, PA, 1856-1884 and Hero Fruit Jar Co., Philadelphia, PA, 1884-1909

H F J Co (in wings of Maltese cross): Hero Glass Works, 1884-1900

HP (close together in circle): Keene Glass Works, Keene, NH, 1817-1822

HS (in a circle): Twitchell & Schoolcraft, Keene, NH, 1815-1816

IDEAL: Hod c. Dunfee, Charleston, WV, 1910

I G Co.: Ihmsen Glass Co., Pittsburgh, PA, 1855-1896

I. G. Co: Ihmsen Glass Co., 1895

I. G. Co.: Monogram, Ill. Glass Co. on fruit jar, 1914

IPGCO: Ill. Pacific Glass Company, San Francisco, CA, 1902-1926

IPGCO (in a diamond): Ill. Pacific Glass Company, San Francisco, CA, 1902-1926

IG: Illinois Glass, F inside a jar outline, C. L. Flaccus 1/2 glass 1/2 co., Pittsburgh, PA, 1900-1928

Ill. Glass Co.: 1916-1929

I G: Illinois Glass Co., Alton, IL, before 1890

I G Co. (in a diamond): Illinois Glass Co., Alton, IL, 1900-1916

Improved G E M: Hero Glass Works, Philadelphia, PA, 1868

I P G: Illinois Pacific Glass Co. San Francisco, CA, 1902-1932

I X L: I X L Glass Bottle Co., Inglewood, CA, 1921-1923

J (in keystone): Knox Glass Bottle Co. of Miss., Jackson, MS, 1932-1953

J (in square): Jeannette Glass Co., Jeannette, PA, 1901-1922

JAF & Co., Pioneer and Folger: J.A. Folger & Co., San Francisco, CA, 1850-present

J D S: John Duncan & Sons, New York, NY, 1880-1900

J. P. F.: Pitkin Glass Works, Manchester, CT, 1783-1830

J R: Stourbridge Flint Glass Works, Pittsburgh, PA, 1823-1828

JBS monogram: Joseph Schlitz Brewing Co., Milwaukee, WI, 1900

JT: Mantua Glass Works, later Mantua Glass Co., Mantua, OH, 1824

JT & Co: Brownsville Glass Works, Brownsville, PA, 1824-1828

J. SHEPARD: J. Shepard & Co., Zanesville, OH, 1823-1838

K (in keystone): Knox Glass Bottle Co., Knox, PA, 1924-1968

Kensington Glass Works: Kensington Glass Works, Philadelphia, PA, 1822-1932

Kerr (in script): Kerr Glass Manufacturing Co. and later Alexander H. Kerr Glass Co., Portland, OR; Sand Spring, OK; Chicago, IL; Los Angeles, CA, 1912-present

K H & G: Kearns, Herdman & Gorsuch, Zanesville, OH, 1876-1884

KH & GZO: Kearns, Herdman & Gorsuch, 1868-1886

K & M: Knox & McKee, Wheeling, WV, 1824-1829

K & O: Kivlan & Onthank, Boston, MA, 1919-1925

KO – HI: Koehler & Hinrichs, St. Paul, MN, 1911

K Y G W and KYGW Co: Kentucky Glass Works Co., Louisville, KY, 1849-1855

L (in keystone): Lincoln Glass Bottle Co., Lincoln, IL, 1942-1952

L: W.J. Latchford Glass Co., Los Angeles, CA, 1925-1938

Lamb: Lamb Glass Co., Mt. Vernon, OH, 1855-1964

LB (B inside L): Long Beach Glass Co., Long Beach, CA, 1920-1933

L. G. (with periods): Liberty Glass Co., 1924-1946

L-G (with hyphen): Liberty Glass Co., 1946-1954

L G (with no punctuation): Liberty Glass Co., since 1954

L & W: Lorenz & Wightman, PA, 1862-1871

Lightning: Henry W. Putnam, Bennington, VT, 1875-1890

LP (in keystone): Pennsylvania Bottle Co., Wilcox, PA, 1940-1952

L K Y G W: Louisville Kentucky Glass Works, Louisville, KY, 1873-1890

"Mascot, "Mason" and M F G Co.: Mason Fruit Jar Co., Philadelphia, PA, 1885-1890

Mastadon: Thomas A. Evans Mastadon Works, and later Wm. McCully & Co. Pittsburgh, PA, 1855-1887

MB Co: Muncie Glass Co., Muncie, IN, 1895-1910

M B & G Co: Massillon Bottle & Glass Co., Massillon, OH, 1900-1904

M B W: Millville Bottle Works, Millville, NJ, 1903-1930

M. Casey, Gilroy Brewery Cal.: Chicago Bottle Works, San Francisco, CA, 1896-1906

McL (in circle): McLaughlin Glass Co., Vernon, CA, 1920-1936, Gardena, CA, 1951-1956

MEDALLION: M.S. Burr & Co., Boston, MA (mfgr. of nursing bottles), 1874

M (in keystone): Metro Glass Bottle Co., Jersey City, NJ, 1935-1949

MG: Straight letters 1930-1940; slanted letters, Maywood Glass, Maywood, CA, 1940-1958

M. G. W.: Middletown Glass Co., NY, 1889

Moore Bros.: Moore Bros., Clayton, NJ, 1864-1880

MOUNT VERNON: Cook & Bernheimer Co., New York, NY, 1890

N (in keystone): Newborn Glass Co., Royersford, PA, 1920-1925

N: H. Northwood Glass Co., Wheeling, WV, 1902-1925

N (bold N in bold square): Obear-Nester Glass Co., St. Louis, Missouri and East St. Louis, IL, 1895

N 17: American Bottle Co., Toledo, OH, Div. of Owens Bottle Co., 1917-1929

N. B. B. G. Co: North Baltimore Bottle Glass Co., North Baltimore, OH, 1888-1995; Albany, IN, 1895-1900; Terre Haute, IN, 1900-1926

N. Cervelli (N over C in middle) 615 Francisco ST. S.F.: 1898-1906

N G Co: Northern Glass Co., Milwaukee, WI, 1894-1896

N - W: Nivison-Weiskopf Glass Co., Reading, OH, 1900-1931

O (in a square): Owen Bottle Co., 1919-1929

O B C: Ohio Bottle Co., Newark, OH, 1904-1905

O-D-1-O & Diamond & I: Owens Ill. Pacific Coast Co., CA, 1932-1943. Mark of Owens-Ill. Glass Co. merger in 1930

O G W: Olean Glass Co. (Works), Olean, NY, 1887-1915

O (in keystone): Oil City Glass Co., Oil City, PA, 1920-1925

OSOTITE (in elongated diamond): Warren Fruit Jar Co., Fairfield, IA, 1910

O-U-K I D: Robert A Vancleave, Philadelphia, PA, 1909

P (in keystone): Wightman Bottle & Glass Co., Parker Landing, PA, 1930-1951

PCGW: Pacific Coast Glass Works, San Francisco, CA, 1902-1924

PEERLESS: Peerless Glass Co., Long Island City, NY, 1920-1935 (was Bottler's & Manufacturer's Supply Co., 1900-1920)

P G W: Pacific Glass Works, San Francisco, CA, 1862-1876

Picture of young child in circle: M.S. Burr & Co., Boston, MA (mfgr. of nursing bottles), 1874

Premium: Premium Glass Co., Coffeyville, KS, 1908-1914

P in square or pine in box: Pine Glass Corp., Okmulgee, OK, 1927-1929

P S: Puget Sound Glass Co., Anacortes, WA, 1924-1929

Putnam Glass Works (in a circle): Putnam Flint Glass Works, Putnam, OH, 1852-1871

P & W: Perry & Wood and later Perry & Wheeler, Keene, NH, 1822-1830

Queen (in script) Trade Mark (all in a shield): Smalley, Kivian & Onthank, Boston, MA, 1906-1919

Rau's: Fairmount Glass Works, Fairmount, IN, 1898-1908

Ravenna Glass Works: Ravenna Glass Works, Ravenna, OH, 1857-1867

R & C Co: Roth & Co., San Francisco, CA, 1879-1888

Red (with a key through it): Safe Glass Co., Upland, IN, 1892-1898

R G Co.: Renton Glass Co., Renton, WA, 1911s

Root: Root Glass Co., Terre Haute, IN, 1901-1932

S (in a star): Southern Glass Co., L.A., 1920-1929

S (in a circle): Southern Glass Co., 1919-1920

S (in an elongated diamond): Southern Glass Co., 1920-1925

S (in a triangle): Schloss Crockery Co., San Francisco, CA, 1910

S (in keystone): Seaboard Glass Bottle Co. Pittsburgh, PA, 1943-1947

SB & GCo: Streator Bottle & Glass Co., Streator, IL, 1881-1905

SF & PGW: San Francisco & Pacific Glass Works, San Francisco, CA, 1876-1900

S & C: Stebbins & Chamberlain or Coventry Glass Works, Coventry, CT, 1825-1830

S F G W: San Francisco Glass Works, San Francisco, CA, 1869-1876

SIGNET (blown in bottom): Chicago Heights Bottle Co., Chicago, Heights, IL, 1913

Squibb: E.R. Squibb, M.D., Brooklyn, NY, 1858-1895

Standard (in script, Mason): Standard Coop. Glass Co., and later Standard Glass Co., Marion, IN, 1894-1932

Star Glass Co: Star Glass Co., New Albany, IN, 1867-1900

Swayzee: Swayzee Glass Co. Swayzee, IN, 1894-1906

T (in keystone): Knox Glass Bottle Co. of Miss., Palestine, TX, 1941-1953

T C W: T.C. Wheaton Co., Millville, NJ, 1888-present

THE BEST (in an arch): Gotham Co., New York, NY, 1891

TIP TOP: Charles Boldt Glass Co., Cincinnati, OH, 1904

T W & Co.: Thomas Wightman & Co., Pittsburgh, PA, 1871-1895

T S: Coventry Glass Works, Coventry, CT, 1820-1824

U: Upland Flint Bottle Co., Upland, Inc., 1890-1909

U in Keystone: Pennsylvania Bottle Co., Sheffield, PA, 1929-1951

U S: United States Glass Co., Pittsburgh, PA, 1891-1938, Tiffin, OH, 1938-1964

WARRANTED (in arch) FLASK: Albert G. Smalley, Boston, MA, 1892

WARREN GLASS WORKS Co.: Warren Glass Works, 1880-1888

W & CO: Thomas Wightman & Co., Pittsburgh, PA, 1880-1889

W C G Co: West Coast Glass Co., Los Angeles, CA, 1908-1930

WF & S MILW: William Franzen & Son, Milwaukee, WI, 1900-1929

W G W: Woodbury Glass Works, Woodbury, NJ, 1882-1900

WILLIAM FRANK PITTSBURG: William Frank & Sons, Pittsburgh, 1866-1875

WM. FRANK & SONS, PITTS: William Frank & Sons, Pittsburgh, 1866-1875

WYETH: Drug manufacturer, 1880-1910

W. T. & Co. (in rectangle): Whitall-Tatum & Co., Millville, NJ, 1875-1885

W.T. & Co. - E (in small rectangle within big rectangle): Whitall Tatum, Millville, NJ, 1885-1895

W.T. & Co. – C – U.S.A. (in small rectangle within big rectangle): Whitall Tatum, Millville, NJ, 1891-1984

W.T. & Co. – U.S.A. (in small rectangle within big rectangle): Whitall Tatum, Millville, NJ, 1890-1901

W T R Co.: W.T. Rawleigh Manufacturing Co., Freeport, IL, 1925-1936

Museums and Research Resources

Biedenharn Coca-Cola Museum
1107 Washington St.
Vicksburg, MS 39183
Phone: (601) 638-6514
www.biedenharncoca-
    colamuseum.com

Bottle Tree Ranch, The
24266 National Trails Hwy.
Oro Grande, CA 92368

Central Nevada Museum
Logan Field Rd.
P.O. Box 326
Tonopah, NV 89049
Phone: (775) 482-9676
www.tonopahnevada.com/
    centrainevadamuseum.html

Coca-Cola Company Archives
P.O. Drawer 1734
Atlanta, GA 30301
Phone: (800) 438-2653
cocacola.com

Corning Museum of Glass
One Museum Way
Corning, NY 14830-2253
Phone: (607) 974-8271 or
    (800) 732-6845
www.corningglasscenter.com,
    www.pennynet.org/glmuseum

Dr. Pepper Museum
300 S. 5th St.
Waco, TX 76701
Phone: (254) 757-2433
www.drpeppemuseum.com

The Glass Museum
309 S. Franklin
Dunkirk, IN 47336-1209
Phone/Fax: (765) 768-6872

Hawaii Bottle Museum
27 Kalopa Mauka Rd.
P.O. Box 1635
Honokaa, HI 96727-1635

Heritage Glass Museum
25 High St. East
Glassboro, NJ 08028
Phone: (856) 881-7468

Historical Glass Museum
1157 Orange St.
Redlands, CA 92374-3218
Phone: (909) 798-0868
www.historicalglassmuseum.com

**Museum of American Glass
    at Wheaton Village**
1501 Glasstown Rd.
Millville, NJ 08332-1568
Phone: (856) 825-6800 or
    (800) 998-4552
www.wheatonvillage.org

Museum of Connecticut Glass
27 Plank Lane
Glastonbury, CT 06033-2523
Phone: (860) 633-2944
www.glassmuseum.org

National Bottle Museum
76 Milton Ave.
Ballston Spa, NY 12020
Phone: (515) 885-7589
www.crisny.org/not-for-profit/nbm

National Heisey Glass Museum
169 W. Church St.
Newark, OH 43055
Phone: (740) 345-2932

Ohio Glass Museum
124 W. Main St.
Lancaster, OH 43130
Phone: (740) 687-0101
www.ohioglassmuseum.org

Pepsi-Cola Company Archives
One Pepsi Way
Somers, NY 10589
Phone: (914) 767-6000
www.pepsi.com

Sandwich Glass Museum
P.O. Box 103
129 Main St.
Sandwich, MA 02563
Phone: (508) 888-0251
email: sgm@
    sandwichglassmuseum.org

Glossary

ABM (Automatic Bottle Machine): This innovation by Michael Owens in 1903 allowed an entire bottle to be made by machine in one step. ABM bottles are identified by the seam going to the top of the mouth. By 1913 all bottles were manufactured by ABMs.

ACL (Applied Color Label): A method of labeling or decorating a bottle by applying borosilicate glass and mineral pigments with a low melting point to the bottle through a metal screen and baking it in a furnace. The molten glass and pigment form the painted label.

Agate Glass: A glass made from mix incorporating blasting furnace slag. Featuring striations of milk glass in off-white tints, the glass has been found in shades of chocolate brown, caramel brown, natural agate, and tanned leather. It was made from the 1850 to the 1900s.

Amethyst-Colored Glass: A clear glass that when exposed to the sun or bright light for a long period of time turns various shades of purple. Only glass that contains manganese turns purple.

Amber-Colored Glass: Nickel was added in the glass production to obtain this common bottle color. It was believed that the dark color would prevent the sun from ruining the contents of the bottle.

Annealing: The gradual cooling of hot glass in a cooling chamber or annealing oven.

Applied Lip/Top: On pre-1880s bottles, the neck was applied after removal from the blowpipe. The neck may be just a ring of glass trailed around the neck.

Aqua-Colored Glass: The natural color of glass. The shades depend on the amount of iron oxide contained in the glass production. Produced until the 1930s.

Bail: A wire clamp consisting of a wire that runs over the top of the lid or lip, and a "locking" wire that presses down on the bail and the lid, resulting in an airtight closure.

Barber Bottle: In the 1880s, these colorful bottles decorated the shelves of barbershops and were usually filled with bay rum.

Batch: A mixture of the ingredients necessary in manufacturing glass.

Battledore: A wooden paddle used to flatten the bottom or sides of a bottle.

Bead: A raised ridge of glass with a convex section encircling the neck of a bottle.

Bitters: Herbal "medicines" containing a great quantity of alcohol, usually corn whiskey.

Black Glass: A glass produced between 1700 and 1875 that is actually a dark olive-green or olive-amber color caused by the carbon in the glass production.

Blob Seal: A way of identifying an unembossed bottle by applying a molten coin-shaped blob of glass to the shoulder of the bottle, into which a seal with the logo or name of the distiller, date, or product name was impressed.

Blob Top: A lip on a soda or mineral water bottle made by applying a thick blob of glass to the top of the bottle. A wire held the stopper, which was seated below the blob and anchored the wire when the stopper was closed, to prevent carbonation from escaping.

Blown in Mold, Applied Lip (Bimal): A bottle formed when a gather of glass was blown into a mold to take the shape of the mold. The lip on these bottles were added later and the bases often have open-pontil scars. Side seams stop before the lip.

Blowpipe: A hollow iron tube wider and thicker at the gathering end than at the blowing end. The blowpipe was used by the blower to pick up the molten glass, which was then blown in the mold or free blown outside the mold. Pipes can vary from 2-1/2 to 6 feet long.

Blow-Over: A bubble-like extension of glass above a jar or bottle lip blown so the blowpipe could be broken free from the jar after blowing. The blow-over was then chipped off and the lip ground.

Bocca: An opening on the side of the furnace where the pot was placed. The glass batch was placed in the pot where the gather was taken.

Borosilicate: A type of glass originally formulated for making scientific glassware.

Bottom Hinge Mold: A two-piece mold hinged together at the base portion of the mold.

Bruise: Identical to a "fish eye," except that some bruises may be more transparent. A faint bruise is clearer, while a bigger bruise resembles the white eye of a fish.

Bubbles/Blisters: Air or gas pockets that became trapped in the glass during the manufacturing process. The term "seed" is also used to describe these shapes.

Calabash: A type of flask with a rounded bottom. These bottles are known as "Jenny Lind" flasks and were common in the 19th century.

Camphor Glass: A white cloudy glass that looks somewhat like refined gum camphor. This glass was made in blown, blown-mold, and pressed forms.

Carboys: Cylindrical bottles with short necks.

Casewear: Wear marks to the high points of embossing, sides, or base of a bottle due to contact with other bottles in cases while being transported.

Clapper: A glassmaker's tool used in shaping and forming the footing of an object.

Closed Mold: Bottle mold in which the base, body, shoulder, neck, and lip of the bottle all form at one time.

Cobalt Colored Glass: This color was used with patented medicines and poisons to distinguish them from regular bottles. Excessive amounts resulted in "cobalt blue" color.

Codd: A bottle enclosure that was patented in 1873 by Hiram Codd of England. A small ball is blown inside of the bottle. When the ball is pushed up by carbonation, it forms a seal.

Cork Press: Hand tool designed to squeeze a cork into the required shape for use as a bottle closure.

Crown Cap: A tin cap crimped tightly over the rolled lip of a bottle. The inside of the cap was filled with a cork disk, which created an airtight seal.

Cover Groove: A groove on top of the closure or lid that receives the bail and keeps the closure from slipping.

Closed Mold: Bottle mold where the base, body, shoulder, and neck was molded and the majority of the finish conformation was molded.

Crown Cap: A metal cap formed from a tin plate to slip tightly over the rolled lip of the bottle. The inside of the cap was filled with a cork disc, which created an airtight seal.

Cullet: Clean, broken glass added to the batch to bring about rapid fusion to produce new glass.

Date Line: The mold seam or mold line on a bottle. This line can be used to help determine the approximate date a bottle was manufactured.

De-Colorizer: A compound added to natural aquamarine bottle glass to make the glass clear.

Dimple: A small molded depression or hole in a bottle neck where a lever wire or a toggle enclosure is hooked.

Dip Mold: A one-piece mold open at the top.

Embossed Lettering: Raised letters or symbols formed in a mold. They typically identify the maker, contents, and trademark.

Fire Polishing: The reheating of glass to eliminate unwanted blemishes.

Flared Lip: A bottle whose lip has been pushed out, or flared, to increase the strength of the opening. These bottles were usually made before 1900.

Flash: A very faint crack that is difficult to see. The bottle must be turned in a certain position to see the crack.

Flashing: A method of coloring glass by dipping a bottle into a batch of colored glass.

Flint Glass: Glass composed of a silicate of potash and lead. Commonly referred to as lead crystal in present terminology.

Flux: A substance that generates the fusion of glass.

Free-Blown Glass: Glass produced with a blowpipe rather than a mold.

Frosted Glass: Frosting occurs when a bottle's surface is sandblasted.

Gaffer: A term for the master blower in early glasshouses.

Gather: The gob of molten glass gathered on the end of the blowpipe, which the glassmaker then expanded by blowing until it formed a bottle or other glass object.

Glass Pontil: The earliest type of pontil, in which a sharp glass ring remained after the bottle was broken off the pontil rod.

Glory Hole: The small furnace used for the frequent reheating necessary during the making of a bottle. The glory hole was also used in fire polishing.

Gob: A portion of molten glass that is expanded, or blown, into a bottle of other glass vessel, or gathered at the end of a blowpipe.

Green Glass: Refers to a composition of glass and not a color. The green color was caused by iron impurities in the sand, which could not be controlled by the glassmakers.

Ground Pontil: A smooth circular area of glass created after a rough pontil scar has been ground off.

Hobbleskirt: The iconic paneled shape with curved waist used to make the classic Coca-Cola bottle.

Hobnail: Pattern of pressed glass characterized by an all-over pattern of bumps that look like hobnail heads.

Hutchinson Stopper: A spring-type internal closure used to seal soda bottles, patented by Charles Hutchinson in 1879.

Imperfections: Flaws such as bubbles, or tears, bent shapes and necks, imperfect seams, and errors in spelling and embossing.

ISP (Inserted Slug Plate): Special or unique company names, or names of people, were sometimes embossed on ale, whiskey, and wine bottles, using a plate inserted into the mold.

Improved Pontil: Bottles having an improved pontil appear with reddish or blackish tinges on the base.

Iron Pontil: The solid iron rod heated and affixed to a bottle's base created a scar as a black circular depression often turning red upon oxidation. This is also referred to as a bare iron pontil or improved pontil.

Iridescence: A stain found on an old bottle that has been dug from the ground. The stain has an opaline or rainbow color due to the minerals in the ground fusing with the glass. Therefore, this stain is very difficult to clean and usually remains in the glass.

Jack: A steel or wooden tong-like tool the gaffer used to manipulate hot glass.

Keyed Mold: A variation of a two-piece hinge mold, in which the bottom mold seam is not straight but arches up at the middle of the bottle base.

Kick-Up: The deep indentation added to the bottom of a bottle. The indentation is formed by pressing a piece of wood or metal into the base of the mold while the glass is still hot. The kickup is common on wine bottles and calabash flasks.

Laid-On-Ring: A bead of glass that has been trailed around the neck opening to reinforce the opening.

Lady's Leg: A bottle with a long curving neck.

Lehr: An annealing oven or furnace in which a new blown bottle was gradually cooled to increase its strength and reduce cooling breakage.

Lightning Closure: A closure with an intertwined wire bail configuration to hold the lid on fruit jars. This closure was also common with soda bottles.

Lipper: A wood tool used to widen lips and form rims and spouts of pitchers, carafes, and wide-mouthed jars.

Manganese: A mineral used as a decolorizer between 1850 and 1910. Manganese causes glass to turn purple when exposed to ultraviolet rays from the sun.

Melting Pot: A clay pot used to melt silicate in the process of making glass.

Metal: Molten glass.

Milk Glass: White glass formed by adding tin to the molten glass. Milk glass was primarily used for making cosmetic bottles.

Moil: Residual glass remaining on the tip of a blowpipe after detaching the blowpipe from the blown bottle.

Mold, Full-Height Three-Piece: A mold in which the entire bottle was formed in one piece. The two seams on the bottle run from the base to below the lip on both sides.

Mold, Three-Piece Dip: A mold that formed a bottle in three pieces that were later joined together. In this mold, the bottom part of the bottle mold is one piece and the top, from the shoulder up, has two separate pieces. Mold seams appear circling the bottle at the shoulder and on each side of the neck.

Opalescence: Opalescence is found on "frosty" or iridescent bottles that have been buried in the earth in mud or silt. The minerals in these substances have interacted with the glass to create these effects.

Open Mold: A mold in which only the base and body of the bottle is formed in the mold, with the neck and lip being added later.

Open Pontil: The blowpipe, rather than a separate rod, was affixed to the base, leaving a raised or depressed circular scar called a moil.

Owens Automatic Bottle Machine: The first automatic glass-blowing machine was patented in 1904 by Michael Owens of the Libby Glass Company, Toledo, Ohio,

Painted Label: Abbreviation for Applied Color Label (ACL), which is baked on the outside of the bottle and was used commonly used on soda pop and milk bottles.

Panelled: A bottle that isn't circular or oval and that is made with four to twelve panels.

Paste Mold: A mold made of two or more pieces of iron and coated with a paste to prevent scratches on the glass, thereby eliminating the seams as the glass was turned in the mold.

Pattern Molded: Glass that was formed into a pattern before being completed.

Plate Glass: Pure glass comprised of lime and soda silicate.

Pontil, Puntee, or Punty Rod: The iron rod attached to the base of a bottle by a gob of glass to hold the bottle during the finishing.

Pontil Mark: A glass scar on the bottom of a bottle formed when the bottle was broken off the pontil rod. To remove a bottle from a blowpipe, an iron pontil rod with a small amount of molten glass was attached to the bottom of the bottle. A sharp tap removed the bottle from the pontil rod, leaving the scar.

Potstones: Flaws resembling white stones created by impurities in the glass batch.

Pressed Glass: Glass that has been pressed into a mold to take the shape of the mold or the pattern within the mold.

Pucellas: Called "the tool" by glassmakers, this implement is essential in shaping both the body and opening in blown bottles.

Pumpkinseed: A small round flat flask, often found in the Western United States. Generally made of clear glass, the shape resembles the seed of the grown pumpkin. Pumpkinseeds are also known as "mickies," "saddle flasks," and "two-bit ponies."

Punt: A term used in the wine bottle trade to describe a kick-up or push-up at the bottom of the bottle.

Ribbed: A bottle with vertical or horizontal lines embossed into the bottle.

Rolled Lip or Finish: A smooth lip formed when the blowpipe was removed from the bottle. The hot glass at the removal point was rolled or folded into the neck to form and smooth out the top of the finish and to strengthen the neck.

Round Bottom: A soda bottle made of heavy glass and shaped like a torpedo. The rounded bottom ensured that the bottle would be placed on its side, keeping the liquid in contact with the cork and preventing the cork from drying and popping out of the bottle.

Sabot: A type of tool that holds a bottle base for finishing purposes.

Satin Glass: A smooth glass manufactured by exposing the surface of the glass to hydrofluoric acid vapors.

Scant Size: Term for a bottle (normally liquor) referred to as a "pint" or "quart" but that actually held less capacity.

Seal: A circular or oval slug of glass applied to the shoulder of a bottle with an imprint of the manufacturer's name, initials, or mark.

Seam: A mark on a bottle where the two halves meet caused by glass assuming the shape of the mold.

Servitor: An assistant to the master glassblower (gaffer).

Sheared Lip: A plain lip formed by clipping the hot glass of the bottle neck from the bottle using a pair of scissors like shears. No top was applied, but sometimes a slight flange was created.

Sick Glass: Glass bearing superficial decay or deterioration with a grayish tinge caused by erratic firing.

Slug Plate: A metal plate approximately 2 inches by four inches with a firm's name on it that was inserted into a mold. The slug plate was removable, allowing a glasshouse to use the same mold for many companies by simply switching slug plates.

Smooth Base: A bottle made without a pontil.

Snap Case: Also called a snap tool, the snap case had arms that extended from a central stem to hold a bottle firmly on its sides during finishing of the neck and lip. The snap case replaced the pontil rod, and thus eliminated the pontil scars or marks. It sometimes left grip marks on the side of the bottle, however.

Squat: A bottle designed to hold beer, porter, and soda.

Tooled Top: A bottle with a top that is formed in the bottle mold. Bottles of this type were manufactured after 1885.

Torpedo: A beer or soda bottle with a rounded base meant to lie on its side to keep the cork wet and prevent air from leaking in or the cork from popping out.

Turn-Mold Bottles: Bottles turned in a mold using special solvents. The continuous turning with the solvent erased all seams and mold marks and added a distinct luster to the bottle.

Utility Bottles: Multipurpose bottles that could be used to hold a variety of products.

WCF: Wire Cork Fastener.

Wetting Off: Touching the neck of a hot bottle with water to break it off the blowpipe.

Whittle Marks: Small blemishes on the outside of bottles made in carved wooden molds. These blemishes also occurred when hot glass was poured into cold molds early in the morning, which created "goose pimples" on the surface of the glass. As the molds warmed, the glass became smoother.

Wiped Top: A bottle in which the mold lines end before the top due to the neck being wiped smooth after the top was tooled onto the bottle. This method was used before 1915.

Xanthine Glass: Yellow glass achieved by adding silver to the glass batch.

About the Author

Michael Polak is known as the "Bottle King" for good reason. With nearly 40 years in the hobby and with a personal collection of more than 3,000 bottles, Polak is a leading authority on bottle collecting in the United States.

He has written more than 11 books on bottle collecting, including *Antique Trader Bottles Identification and Price Guide*, and has contributed numerous magazine and newspaper articles on the subject. He is a member of the Los Angeles Historical Bottle Club, San Diego Antique Bottle Club, Las Vegas Bottle Club and the Federation of Historical Bottle Collectors.

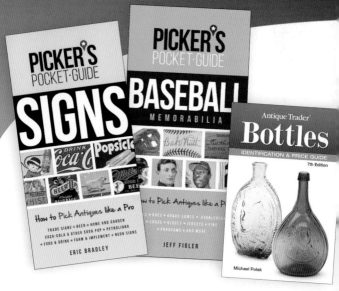